CompTIA® A+
2009 Q&A

CompTIA® A+
2009 Q&A

Chimborazo Publishing, Inc.

Course Technology PTR

A part of Cengage Learning

COURSE TECHNOLOGY
CENGAGE Learning™

Australia, Brazil, Japan, Korea, Mexico, Singapore, Spain, United Kingdom, United States

COURSE TECHNOLOGY
CENGAGE Learning™

CompTIA® A+ 2009 Q&A
Chimborazo Publishing, Inc.

Publisher and General Manager, Course Technology PTR:
Stacy L. Hiquet

Associate Director of Marketing:
Sarah Panella

Manager of Editorial Services:
Heather Talbot

Marketing Manager:
Mark Hughes

Acquisitions Editor:
Megan Belanger

Project/Copy Editor:
Karen A. Gill

Technical Reviewer:
Danielle Shaw

Interior Layout Tech:
Bill Hartman

Cover Designer:
Mike Tanamachi

Proofreader:
Ann Fisher

For product information and technology assistance, contact us at
Cengage Learning Customer & Sales Support, 1-800-354-9706.

For permission to use material from this text or product, submit all requests online at **cengage.com/permissions**. Further permissions questions can be e-mailed to **permissionrequest@cengage.com**.

Microsoft and the Office logo are either registered trademarks or trademarks of Microsoft Corporation in the United States and/or other countries. All other trademarks are the property of their respective owners.

All images © Cengage Learning unless otherwise noted.

Library of Congress Control Number: 2009933323

ISBN-13: 978-1-4354-5490-3

ISBN-10: 1-4354-5490-1

Course Technology, a part of Cengage Learning
20 Channel Center Street
Boston, MA 02210
USA

Cengage Learning is a leading provider of customized learning solutions with office locations around the globe, including Singapore, the United Kingdom, Australia, Mexico, Brazil, and Japan. Locate your local office at: **international.cengage.com/region**.

Cengage Learning products are represented in Canada by Nelson Education, Ltd.

For your lifelong learning solutions, visit **courseptr.com**.

Visit our corporate Web site at **cengage.com**.

Printed in the United States of America
1 2 3 4 5 6 7 11 10 09

ABOUT THE AUTHOR

Chimborazo Publishing, Inc. specializes in providing ancillary materials for textbooks at the high school, college, and trade levels, focusing primarily on computer science and information science textbooks. These materials comprise a variety of components, including Instructor's Manuals, PowerPoint presentations, test banks, and distance learning content. Chimborazo specialists have extensive experience through a combination of university courses, industry experience, and teaching. All Chimborazo employees have completed an MA/MS or Ph.D. in computer or information science.

CONTENTS

PART III: COMPTIA A+ EXAM ANSWERS

Part I

CompTIA A+
220-701
Essentials Exam

Domain 1.0 Hardware

Domain 2.0 Troubleshooting, Repair, and Maintenance

Domain 3.0 Operating Systems and Software

Domain 4.0 Networking

Domain 5.0 Security

Domain 6.0 Operational Procedure

HARDWARE

1. What is the most commonly used form factor today?

   A. DIP

   B. ATX

   C. NLX

   D. POST

   220-701 A+ Objective 1.2, "Explain motherboard components, types, and features"

2. The first ATX power supplies and motherboards used a single power connector. What is the name of this connector?

   A. Transformer

   B. Transistor

   C. Resistor

   D. P1 connector

   220-701 A+ Objective 1.2, "Explain motherboard components, types, and features"

3. Which of the following, if supported by the operating system, can turn off the power to a system after the shutdown procedure is done?

   A. Soft switch

   B. Joule

   C. Riser card

   D. P1 connector

   220-701 A+ Objective 1.2, "Explain motherboard components, types, and features"

4. What form factor is a major variation of ATX and addresses some technologies that have emerged since the original development of ATX?

   A. Soft switch

   B. MicroATX

   C. NLX

   D. POST

   220-701 A+ Objective 1.2, "Explain motherboard components, types, and features"

5. What reduces the total cost of a system by reducing the number of expansion slots on the motherboard, reducing the power supplied to the board, and allowing for a smaller case size?

   A. NLX

   B. MicroATX

   C. FlexATX

   D. BTX

   220-701 A+ Objective 1.2, "Explain motherboard components, types, and features"

6. Which of the following is commonly used in slimline and all-in-one cases but can fit into any FlexATX, MicroATX, or ATX case that follows the ATX 2.03 or higher standard?

   A. PicoBTX

   B. NLX

   C. FlexATX

   D. BTX

   220-701 A+ Objective 1.2, "Explain motherboard components, types, and features"

7. What form factor was designed by Intel in 2003 for flexibility and can be used by everything from large tower systems to those ultra-small systems that sit under a monitor?

   A. BTX

   B. MicroATX

   C. FlexATX

   D. P1 connector

   220-701 A+ Objective 1.2, "Explain motherboard components, types, and features"

8. Which of the following designs focuses on reducing heat with better airflow and improved fans and coolers?

   A. BTX

   B. MicroATX

   C. FlexATX

   D. NLX

   220-701 A+ Objective 1.2, "Explain motherboard components, types, and features"

9. What form factor for low-end personal computer motherboards was developed by Intel in 1998 to improve on an older and similar form factor, called the LPX form factor?

   A. BTX

   B. MicroATX

   C. FlexATX

   D. NLX

   220-701 A+ Objective 1.2, "Explain motherboard components, types, and features"

1

10. What is located on the edge of an NLX motherboard?

A. Diode

B. Riser card

C. Joule

D. Inverter

220-701 A+ Objective 1.2, "Explain motherboard components, types, and features"

11. What houses the power supply, motherboard, expansion cards, and drives?

A. Capacitor

B. Riser card

C. Transformer

D. Computer case

220-701 A+ Objective 1.2, "Explain motherboard components, types, and features"

12. What is the name of the first LGA socket?

A. LGA1366 socket

B. PGA 66 socket

C. LGA775 socket

D. SPGA1336 socket

220-701 A+ Objective 1.2, "Explain motherboard components, types, and features"

13. Which statement is true?

A. The X58 chipset supports the Intel LGA1366 socket, the Core i7 processors, and PCI Express Version 2.

B. The X58 chipset has the ability to control memory.

C. The X75 chipset supports the Pentium Extreme Edition processor, multiple video cards, and up to 8 GB of memory.

D. The P25 chipset supports up to 8 GB of DDR3 or DDR2 memory.

220-701 A+ Objective 1.2, "Explain motherboard components, types, and features"

14. What name is used to describe a bus that does not run in sync with the system clock?

A. Sector

B. Jumper

C. Joule

D. Expansion bus

220-701 A+ Objective, "1.2 Explain motherboard components, types, and features"

15. Which statement is true?

A. The frequency state is a command to the processor to wait for slower devices to catch up.

B. The first PCI bus had a 32-bit data path, supplied 5 V of power to an expansion card, and operated at 33 MHz.

C. A Universal PCI card uses a 3.3-V only.

D. PCI- X introduced the 64-bit, 3.3-V PCI slot.

220-701 A+ Objective 1.2, "Explain motherboard components, types, and features"

16. What term is sometimes used interchangeably with throughput?
    A. Boot loader
    B. CrossFire
    C. Bandwidth
    D. Latency
    220-701 A+ Objective 1.2, "Explain motherboard components, types, and features"

17. Which of the following is focused on technologies that target the server market?
    A. PCI-X
    B. PCI Express
    C. AGP
    D. AMR
    220-701 A+ Objective 1.2, "Explain motherboard components, types, and features"

18. What slot contains a single lane for data, which is actually four wires?
    A. PCI Express x16
    B. PCI Express x8
    C. PCI Express x1
    D. PCI Express x4
    220-701 A+ Objective 1.2, "Explain motherboard components, types, and features"

19. Which statement is false?
    A. The original PCIe allowed for 150 W.
    B. PCIe Version 1.1 increased the wattage to 225 watts by allowing two 6-pin connectors from the power supply to the card.
    C. PCIe Version 2 tripled the frequency of the PCIe bus.
    D. PCIe Version 2 also allows for up to 32 lanes on one slot.
    220-701 A+ Objective 1.2, "Explain motherboard components, types, and features"

20. Which statement is false?
    A. A motherboard will have a PCI Express x16 slot or an AGP slot but not both.
    B. AGP has mostly been replaced by PCI Express.
    C. AGP standards include three major releases (AGP 1.0, AGP 2.0, and AGP 3.0)
    D. You can only use a riser card in an NLX system.
    220-701 A+ Objective 1.2, "Explain motherboard components, types, and features"

21. Which statement is false?
    A. If an AGP video card does not use the extra pins provided by the AGP Pro slot, it can still be inserted into the AGP Pro slot if it has a registration tab that fits into the end of the Pro slot near the center of the motherboard.
    B. APG 3.0 cards can be installed in an AGP 1.5-V slot. Signals are also put on the data bus using 1.5 V.
    C. A universal AGP video card can fit into a universal AGP slot.
    D. An AGP video card will be keyed to 1.5 V or 3.3 V.
    220-701 A+ Objective 1.2, "Explain motherboard components, types, and features"

22. What card has part of its audio, modem, or networking logic on the card and part on a controller on the motherboard?
    A. CNR
    B. Ethernet
    C. Riser
    D. PCI
    220-701 A+ Objective 1.2, "Explain motherboard components, types, and features"

23. Which statement is false?
    A. An ACR slot looks like a PCI slot, but it sits a little closer to the rear of the motherboard than does a PCI slot.
    B. ACR cards might be used for wireless or wired networking, FireWire, or modems.
    C. A CNR slot is larger than a PCI slot but about the same height.
    D. AMR and CNR slots are rarely used today, and it's next to impossible to find the cards that fit them.
    220-701 A+ Objective 1.2, "Explain motherboard components, types, and features"

24. What name is used to describe ports that come directly off the motherboard?
    A. Jumpers
    B. Joules
    C. I/O shields
    D. On-board ports
    220-701 A+ Objective 1.2, "Explain motherboard components, types, and features"

25. Which of the following might have several internal connectors, including parallel ATA connectors (also called EIDE connectors), a floppy drive connector, serial ATA connectors, SCSI connectors, or a FireWire (IEEE 1394) connector?
    A. Joule
    B. Motherboard
    C. I/O shields
    D. On-board ports
    220-701 A+ Objective 1.2, "Explain motherboard components, types, and features"

26. What program can easily make changes to the setup values stored in CMOS RAM?

    A. BIOS setup

    B. Ntldr

    C. CMOS

    D. I/O shield

    220-701 A+ Objective 1.2, "Explain motherboard components, types, and features"

27. Some older motherboards and expansion cards store setup data using which of the following?

    A. Scalable Link Interface

    B. Accelerated Graphics Port

    C. Dual inline package (DIP) switch

    D. Staggered pin grid array

    220-701 A+ Objective 1.2, "Explain motherboard components, types, and features"

28. Which statement is false?

    A. A DIP switch has an ON position and an OFF position.

    B. If you add or remove equipment, you can communicate that to the computer by changing a DIP switch setting.

    C. When you change a DIP switch setting, you should use a pointed instrument such as a ballpoint pen to push the switch.

    D. You must replace the entire motherboard if one port fails.

    220-701 A+ Objective 1.2, "Explain motherboard components, types, and features"

29. Which of the following is considered open or closed based on whether a cover is present on two small posts or metal pins that stick up off the motherboard?

    A. Partition table

    B. MBR

    C. Jumpers

    D. On-board ports

    220-701 A+ Objective 1.2, "Explain motherboard components, types, and features"

30. Which statement is false?

    A. A jumper is closed if the cover is in place, connecting the two pins that make up the jumper.

    B. Setup information about the BIOS can be stored by setting a jumper on (closed) or off (open).

    C. A jumper is open if the cover is not in place.

    D. Computers today store most configuration information in CMOS RAM.

    220-701 A+ Objective 1.2, "Explain motherboard components, types, and features"

31. What term refers to the computer bringing itself up to a working state without the user having to do anything but press the on button?

    A. Booting

    B. Defragmenting

    C. Partitioning

    D. Standoff

    220-701 A+ Objective 1.2, "Explain motherboard components, types, and features"

32. Which of the following involves turning on the power with the on/off switch?

    A. Hard boot

    B. Defragmenting

    C. Soft boot

    D. Standoff

    220-701 A+ Objective 1.2, "Explain motherboard components, types, and features"

33. Which of the following involves using the operating system to reboot?

    A. Hard boot

    B. Cold boot

    C. Soft boot

    D. Standoff

    220-701 A+ Objective 1.2, "Explain motherboard components, types, and features"

34. What term describes programming contained on the firmware chip on the motherboard that is responsible for getting a system up and going and finding an OS to load?

    A. I/O shield

    B. Startup BIOS

    C. CMOS

    D. Ethernet

    220-701 A+ Objective 1.2, "Explain motherboard components, types, and features"

35. Which of the following surveys hardware resources and needs and assigns system resources to meet those needs?

    A. CMOS

    B. Startup BIOS

    C. Ethernet

    D. MBR

    220-701 A+ Objective 1.2, "Explain motherboard components, types, and features"

36. Which of the following begins the startup process by reading configuration information stored primarily in CMOS RAM and then compares the information to the hardware: the processor, video slot, PCI slots, hard drive, and so on?

    A. MBR

    B. Startup BIOS

    C. CMOS

    D. BootMgr

    220-701 A+ Objective 1.2, "Explain motherboard components, types, and features"

37. Which of the following can be found at the beginning of the boot drive (usually drive C)?

    A. Ntldr

    B. Startup BIOS

    C. Riser card

    D. OS boot record

    220-701 A+ Objective 1.2, "Explain motherboard components, types, and features"

38. What contains a small program that points to a larger OS program file that is responsible for starting the OS load?

    A. Ntldr

    B. Startup BIOS

    C. BootMgr

    D. Boot record

    220-701 A+ Objective 1.2, "Explain motherboard components, types, and features"

39. Which of the following contains a list of instructions stored in a file?

    A. Ntldr

    B. Program file

    C. BootMgr

    D. Boot record

    220-701 A+ Objective 1.2, "Explain motherboard components, types, and features"

40. What does the OS boot record program point to in Windows Vista?

    A. BootMgr

    B. Program file

    C. Ntldr

    D. Boot record

    220-701 A+ Objective 1.2, "Explain motherboard components, types, and features"

41. For Windows XP, Ntldr is responsible for loading the OS and is therefore called which of the following?

    A. BootMgr

    B. Program file

    C. Boot loader program

    D. Boot record

    220-701 A+ Objective 1.2, "Explain motherboard components, types, and features"

42. What are two standards for the interface between firmware on the motherboard and the operating system?

    A. UEFI and GPT

    B. BIOS and EFI

    C. MBR and GPT

    D. EFI and UEFI

    220-701 A+ Objective 1.2, "Explain motherboard components, types, and features"

43. What disk partitioning system can support up to 128 partitions?

    A. Ntldr

    B. GPT

    C. UEFI

    D. EFI

    220-701 A+ Objective 1.2, "Explain motherboard components, types, and features"

44. What are the three basic components of a processor?

    A. A register, the CPU, and a backside bus

    B. An input/output unit, the CPU, and a backside bus

    C. An input/output unit, a control unit, and one or more arithmetic logic units (ALUs)

    D. A control unit, a register, and a backside bus

    220-701 A+ Objective 1.4, "Explain the purpose and characteristics of CPUs and their features"

45. Which of the following holds counters, data, instructions, and addresses that the ALU is currently processing?

    A. Registers

    B. Buses

    C. Control unit

    D. ALU

    220-701 A+ Objective 1.4, "Explain the purpose and characteristics of CPUs and their features"

46. What term is used to describe the portion of the internal bus that connects the processor to the internal memory cache?

    A. Front–side bus

    B. Internal bus

    C. Left–side bus

    D. Back–side bus

    220-701 A+ Objective 1.4, "Explain the purpose and characteristics of CPUs and their features"

47. What term is used to describe the speed at which the processor operates internally?

    A. Multiplier

    B. Processor frequency

    C. Overclocking

    D. Throttling

    220-701 A+ Objective 1.4, "Explain the purpose and characteristics of CPUs and their features"

48. What occurs when you run a motherboard or processor at a higher speed than the manufacturer suggests?

    A. Cooling

    B. Multiprocessing

    C. Overclocking

    D. Throttling

    220-701 A+ Objective 1.4, "Explain the purpose and characteristics of CPUs and their features"

49. What sits on top of the processor and consists of a fan and a heat sink?

    A. Cooler

    B. Triple core

    C. Dual core

    D. Quad core

    220-701 A+ Objective 1.5, "Explain cooling methods and devices"

50. Which of the following is a heat sink carrying an electrical charge that causes it to act as an electrical thermal transfer device?

    A. Liquid cooling system

    B. Peltier

    C. Water cooler

    D. Fan

    220-701 A+ Objective 1.5, "Explain cooling methods and devices"

1

51. What is the most popular method of cooling overclocked processors?

A. Liquid cooling system

B. Peltier

C. Water cooler

D. Fan

220-701 A+ Objective 1.5, "Explain cooling methods and devices"

52. Which of the following has one notch and uses 184 pins? Instead of processing data for each beat of the system clock, it processes data when the beat rises and again when it falls, doubling the data rate of memory.

A. SIMM

B. ROM

C. DDR

D. SDRAM

220-701 A+ Objective 1.6, "Compare and contrast memory types, characteristics, and their purpose"

53. What comes in two sizes for personal computers: the 2.5-inch size used for laptop computers, and the 3.5-inch size used for desktops?

A. Host adapter

B. Hard drive

C. RAID

D. Floppy disc drive

220-701 A+ Objective 1.1, "Categorize storage devices and backup media"

54. What has one, two, or more platters, or disks, that stack together and spin in unison inside a sealed metal housing that contains firmware to control reading and writing data to the drive and to communicate with the motherboard?

A. Terminating resistor

B. Host adapter

C. Magnetic hard drive

D. Actuator

220-701 A+ Objective 1.1, "Categorize storage devices and backup media"

55. Inside a hard drive, all the read/write heads are controlled by which of the following?

A. Inverter

B. Capacitor

C. Magnetic hard drive

D. Actuator

220-701 A+ Objective 1.1, "Categorize storage devices and backup media"

56. What term is used to describe each side, or surface, of one hard drive platter?

    A. Head

    B. Face

    C. Arm

    D. Actuator

    220-701 A+ Objective 1.1, "Categorize storage devices and backup media"

57. What interface standard defines how hard drives and other drives such as CD, DVD, tape, and Blu-ray drives interface with a computer system?

    A. DMA

    B. ATA

    C. ANSI

    D. S.M.A.R.T.

    220-701 A+ Objective 1.2, "Explain motherboard components, types, and features"

58. What system BIOS feature monitors hard drive performance, disk spin up time, temperature, distance between the head and the disk, and other mechanical activities of the drive to predict when the drive is likely to fail?

    A. DMA

    B. ATA

    C. S.M.A.R.T

    D. ANSI

    220-701 A+ Objective 1.2, "Explain motherboard components, types, and features"

59. What standard allows for one or two IDE connectors on a motherboard, each using a 40-pin data cable?

    A. ANSI

    B. Parallel ATA

    C. ATAPI

    D. IEEE

    220-701 A+ Objective 1.2, "Explain motherboard components, types, and features"

60. Which statement is false?

    A. The 80-conductor IDE cable has 40 pins and 40 wires.

    B. An EIDE drive such as a CD or DVD drive must follow the ATAPI (Advanced Technology Attachment Packet Interface) standard to connect to a system using an IDE connector.

    C. There are five PIO modes used by hard drives.

    D. All motherboards today support Ultra DMA.

    220-701 A+ Objective 1.2, "Explain motherboard components, types, and features"

61. What transfers data directly from the drive to memory without involving the CPU?

    A. ANSI

    B. SATA

    C. PIO

    D. DMA

    220-701 A+ Objective 1.2, "Explain motherboard components, types, and features"

62. Which statement is false?

    A. SATA uses a serial data path rather than the traditional parallel data path.

    B. PATA interfaces are much faster than Serial ATA interfaces and are used by all types of drives, including hard drives, CD, DVD, Blu-ray, and tape drives.

    C. A motherboard can have two, four, six, or more SATA connectors.

    D. SATA supports hot-swapping.

    220-701 A+ Objective 1.2, "Explain motherboard components, types, and features"

63. What is up to six times faster than USB or FireWire?

    A. PATA

    B. SATA

    C. eSATA

    D. ATA

    220-701 A+ Objective 1.2, "Explain motherboard components, types, and features"

64. If a motherboard does not have an embedded SCSI controller, what term is used to describe the gateway from the SCSI bus to the system bus?

    A. Hybrid hard drive

    B. Magnetic hard drive

    C. SCSI host adapter card

    D. Boot sector

    220-701 A+ Objective 1.9, "Summarize the function and types of adapter cards"

65. Which of the following can support both internal and external SCSI devices, using one connector on the card for a ribbon cable or round cable to connect to internal devices, and an external port that supports external devices?

    A. Head

    B. Bus

    C. Host adapter

    D. Connector

    220-701 A+ Objective 1.9, "Summarize the function and types of adapter cards"

66. Each device on a bus is assigned a number from 0 to 15 by means of DIP switches, dials on the device, or software settings. What term is used to identify this number?

    A. Switch ID

    B. SCSI ID

    C. Host adapter

    D. Connector ID

    220-701 A+ Objective 1.9, "Summarize the function and types of adapter cards"

67. To reduce the amount of electrical "noise," or interference, on a SCSI cable, each end of the SCSI chain has which of the following?

    A. Terminating resistor

    B. Fibre Channel

    C. Clamp

    D. Cork

    220-701 A+ Objective 1.9, "Summarize the function and types of adapter cards"

68. What term is used to describe a technology that configures two or more hard drives to work together as an array of drives?

    A. Terminating resistor

    B. RAID

    C. Host adapter

    D. Fibre Channel

    220-701 A+ Objective 1.2, "Explain motherboard components, types, and features"

69. Which of the following terms is used to describe the computer's ability to respond to a fault or catastrophe, such as a hardware failure or power outage?

    A. Terminating resistor

    B. RAID

    C. Host adapter

    D. Fault tolerance

    220-701 A+ Objective 1.2, "Explain motherboard components, types, and features"

70. Which of the following uses space from two or more physical disks to increase the disk space available for a single volume?

    A. RAID 0

    B. RAID 1

    C. RAID 5

    D. RAID 6

    220-701 A+ Objective 1.2, "Explain motherboard components, types, and features"

1

71. Which of the following is referred to, by Windows, as a striped volume?
    A. RAID 0
    B. RAID 1
    C. RAID 5
    D. RAID 6
    220-701 A+ Objective 1.2, "Explain motherboard components, types, and features"

72. Which of the following duplicates data on one drive to another drive and is used for fault tolerance?
    A. RAID 0
    B. RAID 1
    C. RAID 5
    D. RAID 6
    220-701 A+ Objective 1.2, "Explain motherboard components, types, and features"

73. Which of the following is a duplication of everything written to a hard drive?
    A. MBR
    B. Boot sector
    C. Drive image
    D. Mirrored volume
    220-701 A+ Objective 1.2, "Explain motherboard components, types, and features"

74. Which statement is true?
    A. Windows calls RAID 0 a mirrored volume.
    B. Windows calls RAID 1 a mirrored volume.
    C. Windows calls RAID 4 a mirrored volume.
    D. Windows calls RAID 5 a mirrored volume.
    220-701 A+ Objective 1.2, "Explain motherboard components, types, and features"

75. Which of the following stripes data across three or more drives and uses parity checking?
    A. RAID 0
    B. RAID 1
    C. RAID 5
    D. RAID 6
    220-701 A+ Objective 1.2, "Explain motherboard components, types, and features"

76. What contains information about how a floppy disk is organized and which file system is used?
    A. MBR
    B. Mirrored volume
    C. Drive image
    D. Boot sector
    220-701 A+ Objective 1.2, "Explain motherboard components, types, and features"

77. Which statement is false?

    A. Under Windows, a hard drive can use either the NTFS or FAT32 file system, but a floppy drive is always formatted using the FAT12 file system.

    B. Each FAT entry lists how each cluster (or file allocation unit) on the disk is currently used.

    C. A 3 1/2-inch high-density floppy disk has 24 entries in the root directory.

    D. Using FAT12, one sector equals one cluster, so every sector or cluster on the disk is accounted for in the FAT.

    220-701 A+ Objective 1.1, "Explain motherboard components, types, and features"

78. Which statement is true?

    A. A USB cable has two wires.

    B. As many as 127 USB devices can be daisy chained together using USB cables.

    C. External SATA (eSATA) is as least twice as slow as USB or FireWire.

    D. Windows Vista does not support Hi-Speed USB.

    220-701 A+ Objective 1.2, "Explain motherboard components, types, and features"

79. What are common names for a peripheral bus officially named IEEE 1394?

    A. DVI-D and DVI-I

    B. IRQ and DV-I

    C. FireWire and i.Link

    D. UART and VGI

    220-701 A+ Objective 1.2, "Explain motherboard components, types, and features"

80. Which statement is true?

    A. IEEE 1394a supports speeds up to 200 Mbps and is sometimes called FireWire 400.

    B. IEEE 1394a can use cables up to 100 meters (328 feet) and uses a 9-pin rectangular connector.

    C. You can use a 1394 cable that has a 6-pin connector at one end and a 2-pin or 3-pin connector at the other end to connect a slower 1394a device to a faster 1394b computer port.

    D. IEEE 1394a supports two types of connectors and cables: a 4-pin connector that does not provide voltage to a device and a 6-pin connector that does.

    220-701 A+ Objective 1.2, "Explain motherboard components, types, and features"

81. What term implies that data is transferred continuously without breaks?

    A. Isochronous data transfer

    B. Native resolution

    C. Noninterlaced

    D. Resolution

    220-701 A+ Objective 1.2, "Explain motherboard components, types, and features"

82. Which statement is false?

    A. A memory bank is the memory a processor addresses at one time and is 64 bits wide.

    B. Double-sided DIMMs that provide two 64-bit banks are said to be dual ranked.

    C. Dual and quad ranks are a method of reducing the overall price of memory in a system, but at the expense of performance.

    D. Because DIMMs use a 64-bit data path, it takes only three DIMMs to provide one memory bank to the processor.

    220-701 A+ Objective 1.6, "Compare and contrast memory types, characteristics, and their purpose"

83. What term is used to describe the controller logic on a motherboard that manages serial ports?

    A. Video Graphics Adapter

    B. FireWire

    C. Universal Asynchronous Receiver-Transmitter

    D. I/O controller card

    220-701 A+ Objective 1.2, "Explain motherboard components, types, and features"

84. Which statement is false?

    A. The EPP port is sometimes called a normal parallel port or a Centronics port.

    B. The UART chip might control an internal modem that uses resources normally assigned to the serial port.

    C. Serial ports conform to the interface standard called RS-232c.

    D. Parallel ports, commonly used by older printers, transmit data in parallel, eight bits at a time.

    220-701 A+ Objective 1.2, "Explain motherboard components, types, and features"

85. Which of the following provides an infrared port for wireless communication?

    A. DV-I

    B. DVI-D

    C. IrDA transceiver

    D. Universal Asynchronous Receiver-Transmitter

    220-701 A+ Objective 1.10, "Install, configure, and optimize laptop components and features"

86. What is the primary output device of a computer?

    A. Keyboard

    B. Monitor

    C. Mouse

    D. Hard drive

    220-701 A+ Objective 1.7, "Distinguish between the different display devices and their characteristics"

87. What is formed at the intersection of the row and column electrodes?

    A. Hub

    B. FireWire

    C. Refresh rate

    D. Pixel

    220-701 A+ Objective 1.7, "Distinguish between the different display devices and their characteristics"

88. What term is used to describe the number of times one screen or frame is built in one second?

    A. Pixel pitch

    B. Interlaced

    C. Screen size

    D. Refresh rate

    220-701 A+ Objective 1.7, "Distinguish between the different display devices and their characteristics"

89. What term is used to describe the diagonal length of the screen's surface?

    A. Pixel pitch

    B. Interlaced

    C. Screen size

    D. Refresh rate

    220-701 A+ Objective 1.7, "Distinguish between the different display devices and their characteristics"

90. What term is used to describe the number of pixels built into the LCD monitor?

    A. Native resolution

    B. Color quality

    C. Viewing angle

    D. Contrast ratio

    220-701 A+ Objective 1.7, "Distinguish between the different display devices and their characteristics"

91. What CRT monitor draws a screen by making two passes?

    A. VGA

    B. Interlaced

    C. Native resolution

    D. Noninterlaced

    220-701 A+ 1.7, "Distinguish between the different display devices and their characteristics"

92. What CRT monitor draws the entire screen in one pass?

    A. VGA

    B. Interlaced

    C. Native resolution

    D. Noninterlaced

    220-701 A+ Objective 1.7, "Distinguish between the different display devices and their characteristics"

93. For CRT monitors, what is a measure of how many pixels on a CRT screen are addressable by software?

    A. Resolution

    B. Interlaced

    C. Pixel

    D. Noninterlaced

    220-701 A+ Objective 1.7, "Distinguish between the different display devices and their characteristics"

94. Whereas a CRT monitor is designed to use several resolutions, an LCD monitor uses only one. What term is used to describe this resolution?

    A. Standard resolution

    B. Super resolution

    C. Native resolution

    D. Refresh rate

    220-701 A+ Objective 1.7, "Distinguish between the different display devices and their characteristics"

95. What supports up to 640 × 480 resolutions, which is a 4:3 ratio between horizontal pixels and vertical pixels?

    A. SXGA

    B. XGA

    C. SVGA

    D. VGA

    220-701 Objective 1.7, "Distinguish between the different display devices and their characteristics"

96. Which of the following supports up to 800 × 600 resolution?

    A. SXGA

    B. XGA

    C. SVGA

    D. VGA

    220-701 A+ Objective 1.7, "Distinguish between the different display devices and their characteristics"

97. Which of the following supports up to 1280 × 1024 resolution and was the first to use a 5:4 ratio between horizontal pixels and vertical pixels?

    A. SXGA

    B. XGA

    C. SVGA

    D. VGA

    220-701 A+ Objective 1.7, "Distinguish between the different display devices and their characteristics"

98. Which of the following supports up to 2048 × 1152 resolution and is used by 23-inch monitors?

    A. SXGA

    B. QWXGA

    C. SVGA

    D. WQXG

    220-701 A+ Objective 1.7, "Distinguish between the different display devices and their characteristics"

99. Which of the following is the standard analog video method of passing three separate signals for red, green, and blue (RGB)?

    A. 5-pin SVGA port

    B. 15-pin VGA port

    C. 2-pin WQXG port

    D. 6 pin SXGA port

    220-701 A+ Objective 1.9, "Summarize the function and types of adapter cards"

100. What is the digital interface standard used by digital monitors such as a digital LCD monitor and digital TVs (HDTV)?

    A. Composite out port

    B. 15-pin VGA port

    C. DVI

    D. S-Video port

    220-701 A+ Objective 1.9, "Summarize the function and types of adapter cards"

101. What port causes the red, green, and blue (RGB) to be mixed together in the same signal?

    A. Composite out port

    B. 15-pin VGA port

    C. DVI

    D. S-Video port

    220-701 A+ Objective 1.9, "Summarize the function and types of adapter cards"

102. Which of the following sends two signals over the cable—one for color and the other for brightness—and is used by some high-end TVs and video equipment?

    A. Composite out port

    B. 15-pin VGA port

    C. DVI

    D. S-Video port

    220-701 A+ Objective 1.9, "Summarize the function and types of adapter cards"

103. Which statement is false?

    A. Video cards have their own processor called a graphics processor unit (GPU) or video processor unit (VPU).

    B. If a motherboard offers a video port rather than using a video card, the GPU is part of the onboard video controller, and RAM on the motherboard is used for video data.

    C. The less RAM installed on the video card, the better the performance.

    D. Most video cards used and sold today use DDR2, DDR3, Graphics DDR3 (GDDR3), or GDDR4 memory.

    220-701 A+ Objective 1.9, "Summarize the function and types of adapter cards"

104. Which statement is false?

    A. An I/O controller card can provide serial, parallel, USB, or game ports.

    B. A FireWire controller card can provide one or more types of FireWire ports.

    C. A video card can use a PCI, PCIe, or AGP slot.

    D. A video card installs in a slot and provides one or two fans used to cool cards in adjacent slots.

    220-701 A+ Objective 1.9, "Summarize the function and types of adapter cards"

105. What file is larger than JPEG files but retains more image information and gives better results when printing photographs?

    A. TIFF

    B. PNG

    C. GIF

    D. Bitmap

    220-701 A+ Objective 1.8, "Install and configure peripherals and input devices"

106. What file is a set of standards used to represent music in digital form?

    A. USB

    B. DIN

    C. MIDI

    D. MP3

    220-701 A+ Objective 1.8, "Install and configure peripherals and input devices"

107. What port allows a notebook to easily connect to a full-sized monitor, keyboard, AC power adapter, and other peripheral devices?

    A. Docking station

    B. Port replicator

    C. CardBus

    D. PCMIA card

    220-701 A+ Objective 1.10, "Install, configure, and optimize laptop components and features"

108. What provides the same functions as a port replicator but also provides additional slots for adding secondary storage devices and expansion cards?

    A. CardBus

    B. PCMCIA card

    C. Port replicator

    D. Docking station

    220-701 A+ Objective 1.10, "Install, configure, and optimize laptop components and features"

109. Which of the following is used by many devices, such as modems, network cards for wired or wireless networks, sound cards, SCSI host adapters, IEEE 1394 controllers, USB controllers, flash memory adapters, TV tuners, and hard disks?

    A. PCMCIA cards

    B. Port replicators

    C. Docking stations

    D. CardBus

    220-701 A+ Objective 1.10, "Install, configure, and optimize laptop components and features"

110. What improved PC Card slots by increasing the bus width to 32 bits, while maintaining backward compatibility with earlier standards?

    A. ExpressCard

    B. Internet card

    C. CardBus

    D. Inverter

    220-701 A+ Objective 1.10, "Install, configure, and optimize laptop components and features"

111. What name is used to describe a device that connects to a cell phone network?

    A. ExpressCard

    B. Internet card

    C. CardBus

    D. Inverter

    220-701 A+ Objective 1.10, "Install, configure, and optimize laptop components and features"

112. Which statement is false?

   A. A notebook can be powered in by using an AC adapter.

   B. A notebook can be powered in by using a battery pack.

   C. Some AC adapters are capable of auto-switching from 110 V to 220 V AC power.

   D. A DMFC initially provides up to 10 hours of battery life, and future versions will provide up to 15 hours of battery life.

   220-701 A+ Objective 1.3, "Classify power supplies types and characteristics"

113. Which of the following is an electrical device that changes DC to AC?

   A. Inverter

   B. Adapter

   C. Modem

   D. Capacitor

   220-701 A+ Objective 1.3, "Classify power supplies types and characteristics"

114. What is the most common pointing device on a notebook?

   A. Monitor

   B. Keyboard

   C. Touch pad

   D. Graphics tablet

   220-701 A+ Objective 1.10, "Install, configure, and optimize laptop components and features"

115. What is a type of electrophotographic printer that can range from a small, personal desktop model to a large, network printer capable of handling and printing large volumes continuously?

   A. Thermal printer

   B. Impact printer

   C. Laser printer

   D. Inkjet printer

   220-701 A+ Objective 1.11, "Install and configure printers"

116. A laser printer can produce better-quality printouts than a dot matrix printer, even when printing at the same dpi, because it can vary the size of the dots it prints, creating a sharp, clear image. What does Hewlett-Packard (HP) call this technology of varying the size of dots?

   A. Resolution Enhancement technology

   B. XML Paper Specification

   C. Graphics Device Interface

   D. PCL

   220-701 A+ Objective 1.11, "Install and configure printers"

117. What uses a type of ink-dispersion printing and doesn't normally provide the high-quality resolution of a laser printer but is popular because it is small and can print color inexpensively?

A. Thermal printer

B. Inkjet printer

C. Impact printer

D. Laser printer

220-701 A+ Objective 1.11, "Install and configure printers"

118. What type of printer creates a printed page by using a mechanism that touches or hits the paper?

A. Thermal printer

B. Inkjet printer

C. Impact printer

D. Laser printer

220-701 A+ Objective 1.11, "Install and configure printers"

119. What type of printer uses a wax-based ink that is heated by heat pins that melt the ink onto paper?

A. Laser printer

B. Solid ink printer

C. Thermal printer

D. Impact printer

220-701 A+ Objective 1.11, "Install and configure printers"

120. What type of printer uses solid dyes embedded on different transparent films?

A. Dye-sublimation printer

B. Solid ink printer

C. Inkjet printer

D. Dot matrix printer

220-701 A+ Objective 1.11, "Install and configure printers"

121. What type of printer uses ink stored in solid blocks, which Xerox calls color sticks?

A. Dye-sublimation printer

B. Solid ink printer

C. Inkjet printer

D. Dot matrix printer

220-701 A+ Objective 1.11, "Install and configure printers"

122. What type of printer connects directly to a computer by way of a USB port, parallel port, serial port, wireless connection (Bluetooth, infrared, or Wi-Fi), IEEE 1394 (FireWire) port, SCSI port, PC Card, or ExpressCard connection?

A. Thermal printer

B. Network printer

C. Local printer

D. Impact printer

220-701 A+ Objective 1.11, "Install and configure printers"

123. What type of printer has an Ethernet port to connect directly to the network?

A. Impact printer

B. Network printer

C. Local printer

D. Thermal printer

220-701 A+ Objective 1.11, "Install and configure printers"

124. How is a network printer identified on the network?

A. By its IP address

B. By its MAC address

C. By its NIC

D. By its Ethernet card

220-701 A+ Objective 1.11, "Install and configure printers"

125. Under Windows Vista, what can be used to limit and control all kinds of printer-related tasks, including the number of printers that can be installed using the Add Printer Wizard, how print jobs are sent to print servers (rendered or not rendered), which print servers the computer can use, and which printers on a network the computer can use?

A. XPS

B. PCL

C. ACL

D. Group Policy

220-701 A+ Objective 1.11, "Install and configure printers"

126. Which statement is false?

A. When you are responsible for a printer, make sure consumables for the printer are on hand.

B. When working with laser printer toner cartridges, if you get toner dust on your clothes or hands while exchanging the cartridge, use hot water to clean it up.

C. When a laser printer is unplugged, internal components might still hold a dangerous electrical charge for some time.

D. For your protection, laser printers use a laser beam that is always enclosed inside a protective case inside the printer.

220-701 A+ Objective 1.11, "Install and configure printers"

127. What type of printer requires the interaction of mechanical, electrical, and optical technologies to work?

    A. Laser printer

    B. Inkjet printer

    C. Dot matrix printer

    D. Impact printer

    220-701 A+ Objective 1.11, "Install and configure printers"

128. During the cleaning stage of laser printing, what cleans the drum of any residual toner?

    A. Brush

    B. Laser beam

    C. Sweeper strip

    D. Control blade

    220-701 A+ Objective 1.11, "Install and configure printers"

129. During the writing stage of laser printing, what discharges a lower charge only to places where toner should go?

    A. Brush

    B. Control blade

    C. Sweeper strip

    D. Laser beam

    220-701 A+ Objective 1.11, "Install and configure printers"

130. During the developing stage of laser printing, what prevents too much toner from sticking to the cylinder surface?

    A. Control blade

    B. Sweeper strip

    C. Laser beam

    D. Brush

    220-701 A+ Objective 1.11, "Install and configure printers"

131. Which statement is false?

    A. Earlier inkjet printers used 300 × 300 dpi, but inkjet printers today can use up to 5760 × 1440 dpi.

    B. Inkjet printers tend to smudge on inexpensive paper, and they are slower than laser printers.

    C. You should use only paper that is designed for an inkjet printer, and you should use a high-grade paper to get the best results.

    D. Photos printed on a laser printer tend to fade over time, more so than photos produced professionally.

    220-701 A+ Objective 1.11, "Install and configure printers"

1

132. What type of printer can burn dots onto special paper, as done by older fax machines, or the printer can use a ribbon that contains the wax-based ink?

A. Thermal printer

B. Dye-sublimation printer

C. Impact printer

D. Laser printer

220-701 A+ Objective 1.11, "Install and configure printers"

133. How would you determine the IP address of a network printer?

A. Look at the back of the printer.

B. Direct the printer to print a configuration page.

C. Print the MAC address.

D. Look at the NIC.

220-701 A+ Objective 1.11, "Install and configure printers"

134. What term is used to describe memory that is in the processor package but not on the processor die?

A. Level 1 cache

B. Level 2 cache

C. Level 3 cache

D. Level 4 cache

220-701 A+ Objective 1.4, "Explain the purpose and characteristics of CPUs and their features"

135. Which of the following statements about processors is false?

A. Current Intel processors work with system buses that run at 1600, 1333, 1066, or 800 MHz. Current AMD processors work with system buses that run at 1800, 1000, or 800 MHz.

B. Processor core frequency is measured in gigahertz, such as 3.2 GHz.

C. AMD's current desktop sockets are AM3, AM2+, AM2, 754, and 940 sockets.

D. Hyper-threading is the ability of a system to do more than one thing at a time.

220-701 A+ Objective 1.4, "Explain the purpose and characteristics of CPUs and their features"

2.0

TROUBLESHOOTING, REPAIR, AND MAINTENANCE

1. What steps would you take to physically protect your computer?
   A. Block air vents on the front and rear of the computer case.
   B. Leave the PC turned off for weeks or months at a time.
   C. In BIOS setup, disable the ability to write to the boot sector of the hard drive.
   D. Move your computer when it is turned on.
   220-701 A+ Objective 2.5, "Given a scenario, integrate common preventative maintenance techniques"

2. Which of the following is *not* considered a proper computer maintenance procedure?
   A. Check that air vents on the computer case or monitor are not blocked by papers, books, drapes, or other obstructions.
   B. Check that air vents on the computer case or monitor are not blocked by papers, books, drapes, or other obstructions.
   C. Verify that chips and expansion cards are not connected too tightly.
   D. Check cables and cords for wear and tear. Look for trip hazards and correct them if necessary.
   220-701 A+ Objective 2.5, "Given a scenario, integrate common preventative maintenance techniques"

3. Which of the following is *not* the best way to maintain a hard drive?
   A. Rearrange noncontiguous parts of files.
   B. Delete unnecessary files.
   C. Run a weak battery test on the hard drive.
   D. Check the drive for errors.
   220-701 A+ Objective 2.5, "Given a scenario, integrate common preventative maintenance techniques"

4. Which of the following is the best way to clean up the start routine?

    A. Make sure the computer is in a proper environment.

    B. Delete temporary files and check the hard drive for errors.

    C. Keep a record of all software, including version numbers and the OS installed on the PC.

    D. Check that air vents on the computer case or monitor are not blocked by papers, books, drapes, or other obstructions.

    220-701 A+ Objective 2.5, "Given a scenario, integrate common preventative maintenance techniques"

5. Which of the following is the best way to maintain your computer's security?

    A. Verify that a personal firewall is configured and running on the computer.

    B. Keep a record of all software, including version numbers and the OS installed on the PC.

    C. Keep a record of all hardware components installed, including hardware settings.

    D. Delete temporary files and check the hard drive for errors.

    220-701 A+ Objective 2.5, "Given a scenario, integrate common preventative maintenance techniques"

6. Under what circumstances would Windows need free space on the hard drive?

    A. To protect a system against malicious attack

    B. To verify the existence of antivirus software

    C. To check the drive for errors

    D. For defragmenting the drive

    220-701 A+ Objective 2.5, "Given a scenario, integrate common preventative maintenance techniques"

7. Which of the following could cause the hard drive to slow down?

    A. System Restore

    B. Fragmentation

    C. Virtual memory

    D. Dynamic volumes

    220-701 A+ Objective 2.5, "Given a scenario, integrate common preventative maintenance techniques"

8. Which of the following rearranges files on the drive into as few segments as possible?

    A. Dynamic volumes

    B. Defragmentation

    C. System Restore

    D. Telnet

    220-701 A+ Objective 2.5, "Given a scenario, integrate common preventative maintenance techniques"

9. Which statement is false?

    A. To fully defragment the drive, 35 percent of the drive must be free.

    B. Defragmenting a hard drive should be done when the hard drive is healthy.

    C. By default, Vista automatically defrags a drive every Wednesday at 1:00 a.m.

    D. Depending on how fragmented the drive and how large the drive, defragmenting it can take less than an hour or as long as all night.

    220-701 A+ Objective 2.5, "Given a scenario, integrate common preventative maintenance techniques"

10. Which of the following is used to search for and repair file system errors?

    A. Scandisk C

    B. Telnet

    C. Chkdsk

    D. FTP

    220-701 A+ Objective 2.5, "Given a scenario, integrate common preventative maintenance techniques"

11. Which of the following searches for bad sectors on a volume and recovers the data from them if possible?

    A. Scandisk C

    B. Telnet

    C. Chkdsk

    D. FTP

    220-701 A+ Objective 2.5, "Given a scenario, integrate common preventative maintenance techniques"

12. What is equivalent to the *Chkdsk C* command?

    A. Fixboot

    B. Expand

    C. Bootcfg

    D. Scandisk C: /R

    220-701 A+ Objective 2.5, "Given a scenario, integrate common preventative maintenance techniques"

13. Which of the following is an extra copy of a data or software file that you can use if the original file becomes damaged or destroyed?

    A. System File Checker

    B. Driver Query

    C. Backup

    D. FTP

    220-701 A+ Objective 2.5, "Given a scenario, integrate common preventative maintenance techniques"

2

14. Windows XP/2000 offers which of the following programs to back up files and folders?

    A. Ntbackup.exe

    B. Telnet

    C. FTP

    D. Defrag

    220-701 A+ Objective 2.5, "Given a scenario, integrate common preventative maintenance techniques"

15. Which statement is false?

    A. Data should be backed up after about every four to ten hours of data entry.

    B. When you perform a backup for the first time or set up a scheduled backup, verify that you can use the backup tape or disks to successfully recover the data.

    C. Keep your backups in a safe place and routinely test them.

    D. Backups of important and sensitive data should be kept on your desk.

    220-701 A+ Objective 2.5, "Given a scenario, integrate common preventative maintenance techniques"

16. When scheduling backups, what option allows the following to occur? *All files selected for backup are copied to the backup media. Each file is marked as backed up by clearing its archive attribute.*

    A. Copy backup

    B. Incremental backup

    C. Full backup

    D. Differential backup

    220-701 A+ Objective 2.5, "Given a scenario, integrate common preventative maintenance techniques"

17. When scheduling backups, what option allows the following to occur? *All files selected for backup are copied to the backup media, but files are not marked as backed up.*

    A. Copy backup

    B. Incremental backup

    C. Full backup

    D. Differential backup

    220-701 A+ Objective 2.5, "Given a scenario, integrate common preventative maintenance techniques"

18. When scheduling backups, what option allows the following to occur? *All files that have been created or changed since the last backup are backed up, and all files are marked as backed up.*

    A. Copy backup

    B. Incremental backup

    C. Full backup

    D. Differential backup

    220-701 A+ Objective 2.5, "Given a scenario, integrate common preventative maintenance techniques"

19. When scheduling backups, what option allows the following to occur? *All files that have been created or changed since the last full or incremental backup are backed up, and files are not marked as backed up.*

    A. Daily backup

    B. Incremental backup

    C. Full backup

    D. Differential backup

    220-701 A+ Objective 2.5, "Given a scenario, integrate common preventative maintenance techniques"

20. When scheduling backups, what option allows the following to occur? *All files that have been created or changed on this day are backed up. Files are not marked as backed up.*

    A. Daily backup

    B. Incremental backup

    C. Full backup

    D. Differential backup

    220-701 A+ Objective 2.5, "Given a scenario, integrate common preventative maintenance techniques"

21. Which of the following is used by Windows Vista and XP to keep backups of critical system files?

    A. System Protection

    B. System Restore

    C. System File Checker

    D. Driver Query

    220-701 A+ Objective 2.5, "Given a scenario, integrate common preventative maintenance techniques"

22. Which term is used to describe the files critical to a successful operating system load?

    A. Mount points

    B. Fragmented files

    C. Batch files

    D. System state data

    220-701 A+ Objective 2.5, "Given a scenario, integrate common preventative maintenance techniques"

23. Which of the following restores the system to its condition at the time a snapshot was taken of the system settings and configuration?

    A. Chkdsk

    B. FTP

    C. System Restore

    D. Telnet

    220-701 A+ Objective 2.5, "Given a scenario, integrate common preventative maintenance techniques"

24. Which of the following creates restore points at regular intervals and just before you install software or hardware?

    A. System Protection

    B. FTP

    C. System Restore

    D. Defrag

    220-701 A+ Objective 2.5, "Given a scenario, integrate common preventative maintenance techniques"

25. Which of the following statements about System Restore is false?

    A. System Restore can recover from errors only if the registry is somewhat intact.

    B. The restore process can remove virus or worm infections.

    C. System Restore will not help you if you do not have restore points to use.

    D. Restore points are kept in a hidden folder on the hard drive.

    220-701 A+ Objective 2.5, "Given a scenario, integrate common preventative maintenance techniques"

26. Which tool makes a backup of the entire volume on which Vista is installed and can also back up other volumes?

    A. Memory Diagnostics

    B. System Protection

    C. System Restore

    D. Complete PC backup

    220-701 A+ Objective 2.5, "Given a scenario, integrate common preventative maintenance techniques"

27. Which statement is false?

    A. The Complete PC backup must be saved to a local device such as an external hard drive or to DVDs.

    B. In the event your hard drive fails or Vista is so corrupted you cannot recover it, you can restore the volume or volumes from your Complete PC backup.

    C. Complete PC backup is available in Vista Starter.

    D. Vista does not keep multiple copies of backups made using the Complete PC backup method.

    220-701 A+ Objective 2.5, "Given a scenario, integrate common preventative maintenance techniques"

28. What Vista tool can you use to quickly identify a problem with memory or eliminate memory as the source of a problem?

    A. Windows RE

    B. Memory Diagnostics

    C. Driver Query

    D. System Restore

    220-701 A+ Objective 2.2, "Given a scenario, explain and interpret common hardware and operating system symptoms and their causes"

29. What Windows Vista and XP utility protects system files and keeps a cache of current system files in case it needs to refresh a damaged file?

    A. System File Checker

    B. Automated System Recovery

    C. System State data

    D. Recovery Console

    220-701 A+ Objective 2.2, "Given a scenario, explain and interpret common hardware and operating system symptoms and their causes"

30. What is a Windows Vista/XP/2000 utility that runs in the background to put stress on drivers as they are loaded and running?

    A. System File Checker

    B. File Signature Verification

    C. Driver Query

    D. Driver Verifier

    220-701 A+ Objective 2.2, "Given a scenario, explain and interpret common hardware and operating system symptoms and their causes"

31. What tool displays information about digitally signed files, including device driver files and application files, and logs information to C:\Windows\Sigverif.txt?

    A. System File Checker

    B. Driver Query

    C. File Signature Verification

    D. Driver Verifier

    220-701 A+ Objective 2.2, "Given a scenario, explain and interpret common hardware and operating system symptoms and their causes"

32. What tool can be used to direct information about drivers to a file, including information about digital signatures?

    A. System File Checker

    B. Driver Query

    C. File Signature Verification

    D. Driver Verifier

    220-701 A+ Objective 2.2, "Given a scenario, explain and interpret common hardware and operating system symptoms and their causes"

33. Which term implies that the computer freezes and must be restarted?

   A. Latency

   B. Data throughput

   C. Native resolution

   D. System lockup

   220-701 A+ Objective 2.2, "Given a scenario, explain and interpret common hardware and operating system symptoms and their causes"

34. What command scans the hard drive for Windows installations not stored in the BCD?

   A. Bootrec /scanOS

   B. Bootrec /rebuildBCD

   C. Bootrec /fixmbr

   D. Bootrec /fixboot

   220-701 A+ Objective 2.2, "Given a scenario, explain and interpret common hardware and operating system symptoms and their causes"

35. What command repairs the boot sector of the system partition?

   A. Bootrec /scanOS

   B. Diskpart

   C. Bootrec /fixmbr

   D. Bootrec /fixboot

   220-701 A+ Objective 2.2, "Given a scenario, explain and interpret common hardware and operating system symptoms and their causes"

36. What command manages partitions and volume?

   A. Bootrec /scanOS

   B. Diskpart

   C. Bootrec /fixmbr

   D. Bootrec /fixboot

   220-701 A+ Objective 2.2, "Given a scenario, explain and interpret common hardware and operating system symptoms and their causes"

37. Which of the following files is a boot-strap loader program?

   A. Ntdetect.com

   B. Bootsect.dos

   C. Ntldr

   D. Boot.ini

   220-701 A+ Objective 2.2, "Given a scenario, explain and interpret common hardware and operating system symptoms and their causes"

38. Which of the following text files contains boot parameters?

    A. Ntdetect.com

    B. Bootsect.dos

    C. Ntldr

    D. Boot.ini

    220-701 A+ Objective 2.2, "Given a scenario, explain and interpret common hardware and operating system symptoms and their causes"

39. Which of the following files is used to load another OS in a dual-boot environment?

    A. Ntdetect.com

    B. Bootsect.dos

    C. Ntldr

    D. Boot.ini

    220-701 A+ Objective 2.2, "Given a scenario, explain and interpret common hardware and operating system symptoms and their causes"

40. Which of the following is a real-mode program that detects hardware?

    A. Ntdetect.com

    B. Bootsect.dos

    C. Ntldr

    D. Boot.ini

    220-701 A+ Objective 2.2, "Given a scenario, explain and interpret common hardware and operating system symptoms and their causes"

41. Which of the following files is required only if a SCSI boot device is used?

    A. Ntdetect.com

    B. Ntoskrnl.exe

    C. Ntbootdd.sys

    D. Boot.ini

    220-701 A+ Objective 2.2, "Given a scenario, explain and interpret common hardware and operating system symptoms and their causes"

42. Which of the following files is a core component of the OS executive and kernel services?

    A. Ntdetect.com

    B. Ntoskrnl.exe

    C. Ntbootdd.sys

    D. Pagefile.sys

    220-701 A+ Objective 2.2, "Given a scenario, explain and interpret common hardware and operating system symptoms and their causes"

43. Which of the following is a virtual memory swap file?

    A. Ntdetect.com

    B. Ntoskrnl.exe

    C. Ntbootdd.sys

    D. Pagefile.sys

    220-701 A+ Objective 2.2, "Given a scenario, explain and interpret common hardware and operating system symptoms and their causes"

44. What are the two main sections in Boot.ini?

    A. [boot loader] and [operating systems]

    B. Multi(0) and Disk(0)

    C. Rdisk(0) and Partition(1)

    D. Multi(0) and Partition(1)

    220-701 A+ Objective 2.2, "Given a scenario, explain and interpret common hardware and operating system symptoms and their causes"

45. Which of the following is used when Windows 2000/XP does not start properly or hangs during the load?

    A. Windows 2000 Emergency Repair Process

    B. System Restore

    C. Recovery Console

    D. FTP

    220-701 A+ Objective 2.2, "Given a scenario, explain and interpret common hardware and operating system symptoms and their causes"

46. What does the Recovery Console allow you to do?

    A. Write-protect a floppy disk.

    B. Enable or disable a service or device driver.

    C. Defragment your hard drive.

    D. Load the Recovery Console and use the Fixmbr and Fixboot commands.

    220-701 A+ Objective 2.2, "Given a scenario, explain and interpret common hardware and operating system symptoms and their causes"

47. Which of the following is designed so that someone cannot maliciously use it to gain unauthorized access?

    A. Windows 2000 Emergency Repair Process

    B. FTP

    C. Recovery Console

    D. System Restore

    220-701 A+ Objective 2.2, "Given a scenario, explain and interpret common hardware and operating system symptoms and their causes"

48. What command displays or changes the current folder?

    A. cd

    B. batch

    C. attrib

    D. cls

    220-701 A+ Objective 2.2, "Given a scenario, explain and interpret common hardware and operating system symptoms and their causes"

49. What command lists files and folders?

    A. cd

    B. batch

    C. attrib

    D. dir

    220-701 A+ Objective 2.2, "Given a scenario, explain and interpret common hardware and operating system symptoms and their causes"

50. What command creates and deletes partitions on the hard drive?

    A. Expand

    B. Diskpart

    C. Attrib

    D. Bcdedit

    220-701 A+ Objective 2.2, "Given a scenario, explain and interpret common hardware and operating system symptoms and their causes"

51. What command rewrites the Master Boot Record boot program?

    A. Fixmbr

    B. Format

    C. Help

    D. Listsvc

    220-701 A+ Objective 2.2, "Given a scenario, explain and interpret common hardware and operating system symptoms and their causes"

52. What command lists all available services?

    A. Fixmbr

    B. Format

    C. Map

    D. Listsvc

    220-701 A+ Objective 2.2, "Given a scenario, explain and interpret common hardware and operating system symptoms and their causes"

53. What command lists all drive letters and file system types?

   A. Fixmbr

   B. Format

   C. Map

   D. Listsvc

   220-701 A+ Objective 2.2, "Given a scenario, explain and interpret common hardware and operating system symptoms and their causes"

54. What command sets the current directory to the directory where Windows 2000/XP is installed?

   A. Rmdir

   B. Systemroot

   C. Set

   D. Listsvc

   220-701 A+ Objective 2.2, "Given a scenario, explain and interpret common hardware and operating system symptoms and their causes"

55. What command displays or sets Recovery Console environmental variables?

   A. Rmdir

   B. Systemroot

   C. Set

   D. Listsvc

   220-701 A+ Objective 2.2, "Given a scenario, explain and interpret common hardware and operating system symptoms and their causes"

56. What command restores the master boot program in the MBR?

   A. Rmdir

   B. Systemroot

   C. Set

   D. Fixmbr

   220-701 A+ Objective 2.2, "Given a scenario, explain and interpret common hardware and operating system symptoms and their causes"

57. What command repairs the OS boot record?

   A. Rmdir

   B. Fixboot

   C. Set

   D. Fixmbr

   220-701 A+ Objective 2.2, "Given a scenario, explain and interpret common hardware and operating system symptoms and their causes"

58. What command is used to view, create, and delete partitions on the drive?

    A. Diskpart

    B. Fixboot

    C. Chkdsk

    D. Fixmbr

    220-701 A+ Objective 2.2, "Given a scenario, explain and interpret common hardware and operating system symptoms and their causes"

59. What command repairs the file system and recovers data from bad sectors?

    A. Diskpart

    B. Fixboot

    C. Chkdsk

    D. Fixmbr

    220-701 A+ Objective 2.2, "Given a scenario, explain and interpret common hardware and operating system symptoms and their causes"

60. Which of the following commands is useful to find your way around the system, such as when you need to know the drive letter for the CD drive?

    A. Delete

    B. Fixboot

    C. Systemroot

    D. Map

    220-701 A+ Objective 2.2, "Given a scenario, explain and interpret common hardware and operating system symptoms and their causes"

61. What command allows you to view and edit the Boot.ini file?

    A. Bootcfg

    B. Expand

    C. Fixboot

    D. Map

    220-701 A+ Objective 2.2, "Given a scenario, explain and interpret common hardware and operating system symptoms and their causes"

62. What should be used only as a last resort because it restores the system to the state it was in immediately after the Windows 2000 installation?

    A. System Restore

    B. Device Driver Roll Back

    C. Windows 2000 Emergency Repair Process

    D. Windows Defender

    220-701 A+ Objective 2.2, "Given a scenario, explain and interpret common hardware and operating system symptoms and their causes"

63. Which of the following uses the same technology as a PC, but with modifications to use less power, take up less space, and operate on the move?

    A. Notebook

    B. Inverter

    C. Tablet PC

    D. Router

    220-701 A+ Objective 2.4, "Given a scenario, explain and interpret common laptop issues and determine the appropriate basic troubleshooting method"

64. What can be voided by opening the case, removing part labels, installing other-vendor parts, upgrading the OS, or disassembling the system unless directly instructed to do so by the service center help desk personnel?

    A. Notebooks

    B. Warranties

    C. Tablet PCs

    D. Sleep timers

    220-701 A+ Objective 2.4, "Given a scenario, explain and interpret common laptop issues and determine the appropriate basic troubleshooting method"

65. What is an example of diagnostic software?

    A. Trackpoint

    B. Stylus

    C. CardBus

    D. PC-Doctor

    220-701 A+ Objective 2.4, "Given a scenario, explain and interpret common laptop issues and determine the appropriate basic troubleshooting method"

66. Which statement is false?

    A. LCD panels on notebooks are fragile and can be damaged fairly easily.

    B. Always hold the notebook by the display panel.

    C. Always use passwords with each Windows user account so that the laptop is better protected when connected to a public network.

    D. Don't connect the notebook to a phone line during an electrical storm.

    220-701 A+ Objective 2.4, "Given a scenario, explain and interpret common laptop issues and determine the appropriate basic troubleshooting method"

67. What is the most common pointing device on a notebook?

    A. Inverter

    B. Port replicator

    C. Digitizer

    D. Touch pad

    220-701 A+ Objective 2.4, "Given a scenario, explain and interpret common laptop issues and determine the appropriate basic troubleshooting method"

68. IBM and Lenovo ThinkPad notebooks use a unique and popular pointing device embedded in the keyboard. What is the name of this device?

    A. TrackPoint

    B. Stylus

    C. Inver/.ter

    D. Touch pad

    220-701 A+ Objective 2.4, "Given a scenario, explain and interpret common laptop issues and determine the appropriate basic troubleshooting method"

69. Which of the following can be used to hand draw?

    A. Inverter

    B. Port replicator

    C. Graphics tablet

    D. Touch pad

    220-701 A+ Objective 2.4, "Given a scenario, explain and interpret common laptop issues and determine the appropriate basic troubleshooting method"

70. Which of the following is popular with graphics artists and others who use desktop publishing applications?

    A. Inverter

    B. Port replicator

    C. Graphics tablet

    D. Touch pad

    220-701 A+ Objective 2.4, "Given a scenario, explain and interpret common laptop issues and determine the appropriate basic troubleshooting method"

71. What tool is used to restore the system state, data, and software from previously made backups?

    A. Ntbackup.exe

    B. ASR

    C. Boot logging

    D. Bootcfg

    220-701 A+ Objective 2.2, "Given a scenario, explain and interpret common hardware and operating system symptoms and their causes"

72. What tool uses events logged to the Ntbtlog.txt file to investigate the source of an unknown startup error?

    A. Ntbackup.exe

    B. Automatic System Recovery

    C. Boot logging

    D. Cacls.exe

    220-701 A+ Objective 2.2, "Given a scenario, explain and interpret common hardware and operating system symptoms and their causes"

73. What tool is used to gain access to a file when permissions to the file are in error or corrupted?

    A. Ntbackup.exe

    B. Cipher.exe

    C. Boot logging

    D. Cacls.exe

    220-701 A+ Objective 2.2, "Given a scenario, explain and interpret common hardware and operating system symptoms and their causes"

74. What tool is used to decrypt a file that is not available because the user account that encrypted the file is no longer accessible?

    A. Compact.exe

    B. Cipher.exe

    C. Boot logging

    D. Cacls.exe

    220-701 A+ Objective 2.2, "Given a scenario, explain and interpret common hardware and operating system symptoms and their causes"

75. What tool can be used with an NTFS file system to display and change the compressions applied to files and folders?

    A. Compact.exe

    B. Cipher.exe

    C. Boot logging

    D. Cacls.exe

    220-701 A+ Objective 2.2, "Given a scenario, explain and interpret common hardware and operating system symptoms and their causes"

76. What tool can be used to access several snap-ins to manage and troubleshoot a system?

    A. Compact.exe

    B. Device Driver Roll Back

    C. Defrag.exe

    D. Computer Management

    220-701 A+ Objective 2.2, "Given a scenario, explain and interpret common hardware and operating system symptoms and their causes"

77. What tool can be used to replace a driver with the one that worked before the current driver was installed?

    A. Compact.exe

    B. Device Driver Roll Back

    C. Defrag.exe

    D. Computer Management

    220-701 A+ Objective 2.2, "Given a scenario, explain and interpret common hardware and operating system symptoms and their causes"

78. What tool can be used to delete unused files to make more disk space available?

A. Disk Cleanup

B. Driver Signing and Digital Signatures

C. Disk Management

D. Device Manager

220-701 A+ Objective 2.2, "Given a scenario, explain and interpret common hardware and operating system symptoms and their causes"

79. What tool can be used to view and change partitions on hard drives and to format drives?

A. Disk Cleanup

B. Driver Signing and Digital Signatures

C. Disk Management

D. Device Manager

220-701 A+ Objective 2.2, "Given a scenario, explain and interpret common hardware and operating system symptoms and their causes"

80. What tool can be used to identify a driver that is causing a problem?

A. Driver Verifier

B. Driver Signing and Digital Signatures

C. Event Viewer

D. Device Manager

220-701 A+ Objective 2.2, "Given a scenario, explain and interpret common hardware and operating system symptoms and their causes"

81. What tool can be used to display and change policies controlling users and the computer?

A. Driver Verifier

B. Group Policy

C. Event Viewer

D. Last Known Good Configuration

220-701 A+ Objective 2.2, "Given a scenario, explain and interpret common hardware and operating system symptoms and their causes"

82. What tool can be used when Windows won't start normally and you want to revert the system to before a Windows setting, driver, or application that is causing problems was changed?

A. Driver Verifier

B. Group Policy

C. Event Viewer

D. Last Known Good Configuration

220-701 A+ Objective 2.2, "Given a scenario, explain and interpret common hardware and operating system symptoms and their causes"

83. What tool can be used to view information about performance to help you identify a performance bottleneck?

    A. Programs and Features window

    B. Performance Monitor

    C. Program Compatibility Wizard

    D. Recovery Console

    220-701 A+ Objective 2.2, "Given a scenario, explain and interpret common hardware and operating system symptoms and their causes"

84. What tool can be used to resolve issues that prevent legacy software from working?

    A. Programs and Features window

    B. Performance Monitor

    C. Program Compatibility Wizard

    D. Recovery Console

    220-701 A+ Objective 2.2, "Given a scenario, explain and interpret common hardware and operating system symptoms and their causes"

85. What tool can be used to uninstall, repair, or update software or certain device drivers that are causing a problem?

    A. Programs and Features window

    B. Performance Monitor

    C. Program Compatibility Wizard

    D. Recovery Console

    220-701 A+ Objective 2.2, "Given a scenario, explain and interpret common hardware and operating system symptoms and their causes"

86. What tool can be used to troubleshoot a Windows XP/2000 startup problem and recover data from the hard drive?

    A. Programs and Features window

    B. Performance Monitor

    C. Program Compatibility Wizard

    D. Recovery Console

    220-701 A+ Objective 2.2, "Given a scenario, explain and interpret common hardware and operating system symptoms and their causes"

87. What tool can be used to run a program using different permissions than those assigned to the currently logged-on user?

    A. Safe Mode

    B. SC

    C. Runas.exe

    D. Software Explorer

    220-701 A+ Objective 2.2, "Given a scenario, explain and interpret common hardware and operating system symptoms and their causes"

88. What tool can be used to stop or start a service that runs in the background?

    A. Safe Mode

    B. SC

    C. Runas.exe

    D. Software Explorer

    220-701 A+ Objective 2.2, "Given a scenario, explain and interpret common hardware and operating system symptoms and their causes"

89. What tool can be used to view and change programs launched at startup?

    A. Safe Mode

    B. SC

    C. Runas.exe

    D. Software Explorer

    220-701 A+ Objective 2.2, "Given a scenario, explain and interpret common hardware and operating system symptoms and their causes"

90. What tool troubleshoots the startup process by temporarily disabling startup programs and services?

    A. System File Checker

    B. SC

    C. Msconfig.exe

    D. System Information

    220-701 A+ Objective 2.2, "Given a scenario, explain and interpret common hardware and operating system symptoms and their causes"

91. What tool is useful when you suspect system files are corrupted, but you can still access the Windows desktop?

    A. System File Checker

    B. SC

    C. Msconfig.exe

    D. System Information

    220-701 A+ Objective 2.2, "Given a scenario, explain and interpret common hardware and operating system symptoms and their causes"

92. What tool is used to display information about hardware, applications, and Windows?

    A. System File Checker

    B. SC

    C. Msconfig.exe

    D. System Information

    220-701 A+ Objective 2.2, "Given a scenario, explain and interpret common hardware and operating system symptoms and their causes"

93. What tool is useful when managing background services such as an e-mail server or Web server?

    A. System Restore

    B. Task Lister

    C. Task Killing Utility

    D. Task Manager

    220-701 A+ Objective 2.2, "Given a scenario, explain and interpret common hardware and operating system symptoms and their causes"

94. What tool is useful when you need to stop a locked-up application?

    A. System Restore

    B. Task Lister

    C. Task Killing Utility

    D. Task Manager

    220-701 A+ Objective 2.2, "Given a scenario, explain and interpret common hardware and operating system symptoms and their causes"

95. What tool monitors activity and alerts you if a running program appears to be malicious or damaging the system?

    A. System Restore

    B. Windows Defender

    C. Windows Recovery Environment

    D. Windows File Protection

    220-701 A+ Objective 2.2, "Given a scenario, explain and interpret common hardware and operating system symptoms and their causes"

96. What tool runs in the background to protect system files and restore overwritten system files as needed?

    A. System Restore

    B. Windows Defender

    C. Windows Recovery Environment

    D. Windows File Protection

    220-701 A+ Objective 2.2, "Given a scenario, explain and interpret common hardware and operating system symptoms and their causes"

97. What tool runs in the background to prevent or filter uninvited communication from another computer?

    A. Windows Firewall

    B. Windows Defender

    C. Windows Recovery Environment

    D. Windows Update

    220-701 A+ Objective 2.2, "Given a scenario, explain and interpret common hardware and operating system symptoms and their causes"

98. Which term is used to describe a language that was developed by Adobe Systems and is used to communicate how a page is to print?

    A. PHP

    B. PostScript

    C. JavaScript

    D. HTML

    220-701 A+ Objective 2.3, "Given a scenario, determine the troubleshooting methods and tools for printers"

99. Which of the following was developed by Hewlett-Packard but is considered a de facto standard in the printing industry?

    A. HTML

    B. PostScript

    C. PHP

    D. Printer Control Language

    220-701 A+ Objective 2.3, "Given a scenario, determine the troubleshooting methods and tools for printers"

100. Text data that contains no embedded control characters is sent to the printer as is, and the printer can print it without processing. What is this data called?

    A. Raw data

    B. PostScript

    C. HTML

    D. Printer Control Language

    220-701 A+ Objective 2.3, "Given a scenario, determine the troubleshooting methods and tools for printers"

3.0

OPERATING SYSTEMS AND SOFTWARE

1. Which of the following manages hardware; runs applications; provides an interface for users; and stores, retrieves, and manipulates files?

    A. Virtual machine

    B. Systray

    C. Registry

    D. Operating system

    220-701 A+ Objective 3.1, "Compare and contrast the different Windows operating systems and their features"

2. Which of the following is an upgrade of Windows 2000 and attempts to integrate Windows 9x/Me and 2000 while providing added support for multimedia and networking technologies?

    A. Windows NT

    B. Windows XP

    C. Windows Me

    D. Line conditioner

    220-701 A+ Objective 3.1, "Compare and contrast the different Windows operating systems and their features"

3. What is the first Windows OS to allow multiple users to log on simultaneously to the OS, each with their own applications open?

    A. Windows Me

    B. Windows 2000

    C. Windows XP

    D. Windows NT

    220-701 A+ Objective 3.1, "Compare and contrast the different Windows operating systems and their features"

4. Which of the following is a major update or fix to an OS occasionally released by Microsoft?
   A. Service pack
   B. Windows 2000
   C. Windows XP
   D. Windows Me
   220-701 A+ Objective 3.1, "Compare and contrast the different Windows operating systems and their features"

5. What are minor updates or fixes that are released frequently by Microsoft called?
   A. Shells
   B. Drivers
   C. Service packs
   D. Patches
   220-701 A+ Objective 3.1, "Compare and contrast the different Windows operating systems and their features"

6. What is Vista's new 3D user interface called?
   A. Aero user interface
   B. User Account Control dialog box
   C. Virtual machine
   D. Briefcase
   220-701 A+ Objective 3.1, "Compare and contrast the different Windows operating systems and their features"

7. Which of the following is a single task, such as the task of printing a file, that the process requests from the kernel?
   A. Aero user interface
   B. Thread
   C. Patch
   D. Service pack
   220-701 A+ Objective 3.1, "Compare and contrast the different Windows operating systems and their features"

8. Which processors are known as x86 processors because Intel used the number 86 in their model number?
   A. 32-bit processors
   B. 46-bit processors
   C. 64-bit processors
   D. 120-bit processors
   220-701 A+ Objective 3.1, "Compare and contrast the different Windows operating systems and their features"

9. Which of the following statements is correct?

   A. Windows XP Professional x64 Edition is a 36-bit OS.

   B. Vista Home Basic is a 24-bit OS.

   C. Home Premium is a 64-bit processor.

   D. Windows 2000 is a 32-bit OS.

   220-701 A+ Objective 3.1, "Compare and contrast the different Windows operating systems and their features"

10. Which of the following statements is correct?

    A. 64-bit applications can run on a 32-bit OS.

    B. A 64-bit OS requires more resources than a 32-bit OS.

    C. A 64-bit OS theoretically can address up to 4 GB of memory.

    D. The term x86 refers to 64-bit processors and to 64-bit operating systems.

    220-701 A+ Objective 3.1, "Compare and contrast the different Windows operating systems and their features"

11. What refers to a 64-bit OS or to 32-bit processors that process 64-bit instructions, such as the Intel Core2 Duo or 64-bit AMD processors? (AMD64 refers specifically to these AMD processors.)

    A. IA64

    B. x86

    C. x86-64

    D. x92

    220-701 A+ Objective 3.1, "Compare and contrast the different Windows operating systems and their features"

12. What refers specifically to 64-bit Intel processors such as the Xeon or Itanium?

    A. IA64

    B. x86

    C. x86-64

    D. x92

    220-701 A+ Objective 3.1, "Compare and contrast the different Windows operating systems and their features"

13. Which of the following is *not* an available option for launching an application?

    A. Use the Start menu.

    B. Use the Search box.

    C. Use Windows Explorer or the Computer window.

    D. Use System Restore.

    220-701 A+ Objective 3.1, "Compare and contrast the different Windows operating systems and their features"

3

14. What is normally located at the bottom of the Windows desktop, displaying information about open programs and providing quick access to others?

    A. Notification area

    B. Registry

    C. Taskbar

    D. Kernel

    220-701 A+ Objective 3.2, "Demonstrate proper use of user interfaces"

15. What is usually on the right side of the taskbar and displays open services?

    A. Registry

    B. Notification area

    C. Taskbar

    D. Kernel

    220-701 A+ Objective 3.2, "Demonstrate proper use of user interfaces"

16. What is a program that runs in the background to support or serve Windows or an application?

    A. Volume

    B. Command

    C. Patch

    D. Service

    220-701 A+ Objective 3.2, "Demonstrate proper use of user interfaces"

17. What is a term used to describe one or more characters following the last period in a filename (such as .exe, .txt, or .avi)?

    A. Shell

    B. Thread

    C. File extension

    D. Service

    220-701 A+ Objective 3.3, "Explain the process and steps to install and configure the Windows OS"

18. Which term indicates how a file is organized or formatted, the type of content the file contains, and what program uses it?

    A. Shell

    B. Thread

    C. File extension

    D. Service

    220-701 A+ Objective 3.3, "Explain the process and steps to install and configure the Windows OS"

19. What is a new security feature introduced with Windows Vista?

A. Briefcase

B. Virtual machine

C. Netbook

D. User Account Control (UAC) dialog box

220-701 A+ Objective 3.1, "Compare and contrast the different Windows operating systems and their features"

20. What are the two types of user accounts in Vista?

A. An administrator account and a standard account

B. An administrator account and a guest account

C. An administrator account and a user account

D. A user account and a standard account

220-701 A+ Objective 3.1, "Compare and contrast the different Windows operating systems and their features"

21. What is the purpose of the UAC box?

A. To monitor network ports

B. To restrict access to the network

C. To prevent malicious background tasks from doing harm when the administrator is logged on

D. To control traffic from users or programs

220-701 A+ Objective 3.1, "Compare and contrast the different Windows operating systems and their features"

22. Which of the following is true if the top of the UAC box is red?

A. Vista does not trust this program and is not happy with your installing it

B. Vista is happy to accept one of its own Windows components to be installed.

C. The program has signed in with Microsoft, and Vista is happy to install it.

D. Vista does not know or trust the publisher.

220-701 A+ Objective 3.1, "Compare and contrast the different Windows operating systems and their features"

23. Which of the following is true if the top of the UAC box is yellow?

A. Vista does not trust this program and is not happy with your installing it.

B. Vista is happy to accept one of its own Windows components to be installed.

C. The program has signed in with Microsoft, and Vista is happy to install it.

D. Vista does not know or trust the publisher.

220-701 A+ Objective 3.1, "Compare and contrast the different Windows operating systems and their features"

3

24. Which of the following is true if the top of the UAC box is green?

    A. Vista does not trust this program and is not happy with your installing it.

    B. The program has signed in with Microsoft, and Vista is happy to install it.

    C. Vista is happy to accept one of its own Windows components to be installed.

    D. Vista does not know or trust the publisher.

    220-701 A+ Objective 3.1, "Compare and contrast the different Windows operating systems and their features"

25. Which of the following is true if the top of the UAC box is gray?

    A. Vista does not trust this program and is not happy with your installing it.

    B. The program has signed in with Microsoft, and Vista is happy to install it.

    C. Vista is happy to accept one of its own Windows components to be installed.

    D. Vista does not know or trust the publisher.

    220-701 A+ Objective 3.1, "Compare and contrast the different Windows operating systems and their features"

26. What does every OS use to manage a hard drive, optical drive, floppy disk, or USB drive?

    A. Executive services and threads

    B. Directories, subdirectories, and files

    C. Device drivers and volumes

    D. System Restore

    220-701 A+ Objective 3.3, "Explain the process and steps to install and configure the Windows OS"

27. When you refer to a drive and directories that are pointing to the location of a file, as in C:\Data\Business\Letter.docx, what are the drive and directories called?

    A. Path

    B. Systray

    C. Root directory

    D. Notification area

    220-701 A+ Objective 3.3, "Explain the process and steps to install and configure the Windows OS"

28. What file extension identifies the file type as a Microsoft Word 2007 document file?

    A. .avi

    B. .txt

    C. .docx

    D. .exe

    220-701 A+ Objective 3.3, "Explain the process and steps to install and configure the Windows OS"

29. In Windows 2000/XP, the user folder is also named after the user account name. Under which folder is this folder created?

    A. %SystemDrive%\Documents and Settings folder

    B. %SystemDrive%\Users folder

    C. %SystemDrive%\My Documents folder

    D. %SystemDrive%\System folder

    220-701 A+ Objective 3.3, "Explain the process and steps to install and configure the Windows OS"

30. Using Explorer or the Computer window, you can view and change the properties assigned to a file. What are these properties called?

    A. Executive services

    B. Patches

    C. File attributes

    D. File extensions

    220-701 A+ Objective 3.3, "Explain the process and steps to install and configure the Windows OS"

31. Vista is the first Windows OS to use indexing for its searches. What is the list of items that is used to speed up a search?

    A. Index

    B. Images

    C. File attributes

    D. Volumes

    220-701 A+ Objective 3.3, "Explain the process and steps to install and configure the Windows OS"

32. Which of the following is a window containing several small utility programs called applets that are used to manage hardware, software, users, and the system?

    A. System Information Utility

    B. Control Panel

    C. Virtual Machine

    D. Task Manager

    220-701 A+ Objective 3.2, "Demonstrate proper use of user interfaces"

33. Which of the following gives a wealth of information about installed hardware and software, the current system configuration, and currently running programs?

    A. Index

    B. Control Panel

    C. File Attributes

    D. System Information Utility

    220-701 A+ Objective 3.2, "Demonstrate proper use of user interfaces"

3

34. Aside from the standard window, what is the other level of Command Prompt window that Windows Vista provides?

    A. Elevated window

    B. Control window

    C. Utility window

    D. Service window

    220-701 A+ Objective 3.2, "Demonstrate proper use of user interfaces"

35. What operating system has the most limited features and is intended to be used in developing nations?

    A. Windows Vista Business

    B. Windows Vista Home Premium

    C. Windows Vista Home Basic

    D. Windows Vista Starter

    220-701 A+ Objective 3.1, "Compare and contrast the different Windows operating systems and their features"

36. What operating system is similar to Windows XP Home Edition and is designed for low-cost home systems that do not require full security and networking features?

    A. Windows Vista Business

    B. Windows Vista Home Premium

    C. Windows Vista Home Basic

    D. Windows Vista Starter

    220-701 A+ Objective 3.1, "Compare and contrast the different Windows operating systems and their features"

37. What operating system is similar to Windows Vista Home Basic but includes additional features such as the Aero user interface?

    A. Windows Vista Business

    B. Windows Vista Home Premium

    C. Windows Vista Home Basic

    D. Windows Vista Starter

    220-701 A+ Objective 3.1, "Compare and contrast the different Windows operating systems and their features"

38. What operating system includes every Windows Vista feature?

    A. Windows Vista Business

    B. Windows Vista Home Premium

    C. Windows Vista Home Basic

    D. Windows Vista Ultimate

    220-701 A+ Objective 3.1, "Compare and contrast the different Windows operating systems and their features"

39. What operating system is an enhanced edition of Windows XP Professional and includes additional support for digital entertainment hardware such as video recording integrated with TV input?

    A. Windows XP Tablet PC Edition

    B. Windows XP Media Center Edition

    C. Windows Me

    D. Windows NT

    220-701 A+ Objective 3.1, "Compare and contrast the different Windows operating systems and their features"

40. What operating system allows you to install a new OS, without disturbing the old one, so you can boot to either OS?

    A. Drive imaging

    B. Disk cloning

    C. Windows Easy Transfer

    D. Dual boot

    220-701 A+ Objective 3.1, "Compare and contrast the different Windows operating systems and their features"

41. What is the name of an unattended installation performed by storing the answers to installation questions in a text file or script?

    A. Boot file

    B. Answer file

    C. Solution file

    D. Installation file

    220-701 A+ Objective 3.3, "Explain the process and steps to install and configure the Windows OS"

42. Which of the following is a copy of the entire volume on which Windows is installed to another bootable medium, such as a CD or USB drive?

    A. Images

    B. Answer file

    C. Drive imaging

    D. Sysprep.exe

    220-701 A+ Objective 3.3, "Explain the process and steps to install and configure the Windows OS"

3

43. Which of the following can be created to make it easier to recover a hard drive from a catastrophic failure or to deploy Windows and applications to many computers in a corporation?

    A. Image

    B. Answer file

    C. Drive imaging

    D. Driver

    220-701 A+ Objective 3.3, "Explain the process and steps to install and configure the Windows OS"

44. What is the original drive image created by first installing Windows and then using the following Windows utility to remove configuration settings, such as the computer name that uniquely identifies the PC?

    A. Active Directory

    B. Loadstate

    C. Scanstate

    D. Sysprep.exe

    220-701 A+ Objective 3.3, "Explain the process and steps to install and configure the Windows OS"

45. Which term refers to software that simulates the hardware of a physical computer?

    A. Disk cloning

    B. Virtual computer

    C. Workgroup

    D. Sysprep.exe

    220-701 A+ Objective 3.3, "Explain the process and steps to install and configure the Windows OS"

46. There are two popular virtual machine programs for Windows. One of these is Virtual PC by Microsoft. What is the other?

    A. VMWare, Inc.

    B. Windows Easy Transfer

    C. User State Migration Tool

    D. Windows Anytime Upgrade

    220-701 A+ Objective 3.3, "Explain the process and steps to install and configure the Windows OS"

47. What is an advantage of an upgrade installation?

    A. You get a fresh start with a system.

    B. All applications and data and most OS settings are carried forward into the new Windows environment, and the installation is faster.

    C. You are assured that the registry and all applications are as clean as possible.

    D. You can choose to format the hard drive first.

    220-701 A+ Objective 3.3, "Explain the process and steps to install and configure the Windows OS"

48. What keeps track of where the partitions are located on a drive, the size of each partition, and which partition is the active partition (the bootable partition)?

   A. Domain

   B. Boot partition

   C. System partition

   D. MBR

   220-701 A+ Objective 3.3, "Explain the process and steps to install and configure the Windows OS"

49. Which of the following is always a primary partition?

   A. Active partition

   B. Active Directory

   C. Domain

   D. MBR

   220-701 A+ Objective 3.3, "Explain the process and steps to install and configure the Windows OS"

50. Which of the following is the active partition of the hard drive?

   A. Boot partition

   B. Domain

   C. System partition

   D. MBR

   220-701 A+ Objective 3.3, "Explain the process and steps to install and configure the Windows OS"

51. Which of the following is the partition where the Windows operating system is stored?

   A. Boot partition

   B. Domain

   C. System partition

   D. MBR

   220-701 A+ Objective 3.3, "Explain the process and steps to install and configure the Windows OS"

52. Which of the following is a reason to use more than one volume on the drive?

   A. The volume needs to be formatted automatically.

   B. You plan to install more than one OS on the hard drive, creating a dual-boot system.

   C. You need to use the NTFS file system.

   D. The volume is less than 20 GB.

   220-701 A+ Objective 3.3, "Explain the process and steps to install and configure the Windows OS"

3

53. Which of the following statements is true?

    A. NTFS uses smaller cluster sizes than FAT32, which means it makes more efficient use of disk space when storing many small files.

    B. NTFS retains four copies of its critical file system data.

    C. FAT32 offers better security.

    D. NTFS does not use as much overhead as FAT32.

    220-701 A+ Objective 3.3, "Explain the process and steps to install and configure the Windows OS"

54. Which of the following supports encryption and disk quotas (limiting the hard drive space available to a user)?

    A. NTFS

    B. Active Directory

    C. FAT32

    D. DOS

    220-701 A+ Objective 3.3, "Explain the process and steps to install and configure the Windows OS"

55. Which of the following supports compression of an entire volume but not compression of individual files or folders?

    A. NTFS

    B. Active Directory

    C. FAT32

    D. DOS

    220-701 A+ Objective 3.3, "Explain the process and steps to install and configure the Windows OS"

56. Which of the following is a logical group of computers and users that share resources where administration, resources, and security on a workstation are controlled by that workstation?

    A. NTFS file system

    B. Windows workgroup

    C. Active Directory

    D. FAT32 file system

    220-701 A+ Objective 3.3, "Explain the process and steps to install and configure the Windows OS"

57. What type of network is managed by each computer without centralized control?

    A. Wide area network

    B. Local area network

    C. Peer-to-peer network

    D. Client/server network

    220-701 A+ Objective 3.3, "Explain the process and steps to install and configure the Windows OS"

58. Which of the following is a group of networked computers that share a centralized directory database of user account information and security for the entire group of computers?

    A. Client/server network

    B. Intranet

    C. Peer-to-peer network

    D. Extranet

    220-701 A+ Objective 3.3, "Explain the process and steps to install and configure the Windows OS"

59. What type of network manages resources with a centralized computer?

    A. Client/server

    B. Extranet

    C. Peer-to-peer

    D. Intranet

    220-701 A+ Objective 3.3, "Explain the process and steps to install and configure the Windows OS"

60. What is the directory database that Windows Server 2008 uses to control a network?

    A. Workgroup

    B. USMT

    C. Sysprep.exe

    D. Active Directory

    220-701 A+ Objective 3.3, "Explain the process and steps to install and configure the Windows OS"

61. What command-line tool works only when the new Windows Vista or XP system is a member of a Windows domain?

    A. Windows Anytime Upgrade

    B. User State Migration Tool

    C. Windows Easy Transfer

    D. Windows Vista Business

    220-701 A+ Objective 3.3, "Explain the process and steps to install and configure the Windows OS"

62. Which command is used to copy the information from the old computer to a server or removable media?

    A. scanstate

    B. slmgr −rearm

    C. convert

    D. loadstate

    220-701 A+ Objective 3.3, "Explain the process and steps to install and configure the Windows OS"

63. What command is used to copy the information to the new computer?

    A. scanstate

    B. slmgr −rearm

    C. convert

    D. loadstate

    220-701 A+ Objective 3.3, "Explain the process and steps to install and configure the Windows OS"

64. After you have installed Vista, what should you do?

    A. Remove service packs.

    B. Verify that you have network access.

    C. Install software.

    D. Boot from the Vista DVD.

    220-701 A+ Objective 3.3, "Explain the process and steps to install and configure the Windows OS"

65. What method is used by Microsoft to prevent unlicensed use of its software so that you must purchase a Windows license for each installation of Windows?

    A. Product activation

    B. Service Pack

    C. System Restore

    D. Sysprep.exe

    220-701 A+ Objective 3.3, "Explain the process and steps to install and configure the Windows OS"

66. What can be used for a clean install on a computer running MS-DOS, but not to perform an upgrade?

    A. Sysprep.exe

    B. Setup

    C. Winnt.exe

    D. Convert.exe

    220-701 A+ Objective 3.3, "Explain the process and steps to install and configure the Windows OS"

67. Which of the following lists all partitions that it finds on the hard drive, the file system of each partition, and the size of the partition?

    A. Sysprep.exe

    B. Convert.exe

    C. Winnt.exe

    D. Setup

    220-701 A+ Objective 3.3, "Explain the process and steps to install and configure the Windows OS"

68. Which of the following lets you view the applications and processes running on your computer, as well as information about process and memory performance, network activity, and user activity?

A. Control Panel

B. Task Manager

C. Telnet

D. FTP

220-701 A+ Objective 3.2, "Demonstrate proper use of user interfaces"

69. Which Task Manager tab lists system services and other processes associated with applications, together with how much CPU time and memory the process uses?

A. Applications

B. Services

C. Processes

D. Performance

220-701 A+ Objective 3.2, "Demonstrate proper use of user interfaces"

70. Which Task Manager tab lists the services currently installed along with the status?

A. Applications

B. Services

C. Processes

D. Performance

220-701 A+ Objective 3.2, "Demonstrate proper use of user interfaces"

71. Which Task Manager tab provides details about how a program uses system resources?

A. Applications

B. Services

C. Processes

D. Performance

220-701 A+ Objective 3.2, "Demonstrate proper use of user interfaces"

72. On the Performance tab of Task Manager, what graph indicates the percentage of time the CPU is currently being used?

A. Physical Memory Usage History

B. Memory

C. CPU Usage History

D. CPU Usage

220-701 A+ Objective 3.2, "Demonstrate proper use of user interfaces"

73. On the Performance tab of Task Manager, what graph shows how much memory has recently been used?

    A. Physical Memory Usage History

    B. Memory

    C. CPU Usage History

    D. CPU Usage

    220-701 A+ Objective 3.2, "Demonstrate proper use of user interfaces"

74. On the Performance tab of Task Manager, what frame indicates how much RAM and virtual memory the core kernel components of Windows are using?

    A. Physical Memory Usage History

    B. Kernel Memory

    C. System

    D. CPU Usage

    220-701 A+ Objective 3.2, "Demonstrate proper use of user interfaces"

75. On the Performance tab of Task Manager, what frame lists Handles (number of running objects used by all processes), Threads (number of subprocesses), Processes (number of running processes), Up Time (time since the computer was last restarted), and Page File (the first number is the amount of RAM and virtual memory currently in use, and the second number is total RAM and virtual memory)?

    A. Physical Memory Usage History

    B. Kernel Memory

    C. System

    D. CPU Usage

    220-701 A+ Objective 3.2, "Demonstrate proper use of user interfaces"

76. Which of the following can be used to find out what processes are launched at startup and to temporarily disable a process from loading?

    A. Event Viewer

    B. MSconfig

    C. Task Manager

    D. Telnet

    220-701 A+ Objective 3.2, "Demonstrate proper use of user interfaces"

77. What console is used to control the Windows and third-party services installed on a system?

    A. Services

    B. Task Manager

    C. Performance Monitor

    D. Computer Management

    220-701 A+ Objective 3.2, "Demonstrate proper use of user interfaces"

3

78. What window consolidates several Windows administrative tools that you can use to manage the local PC or other computers on the network?

A. Task Manager

B. Performance Monitor

C. Computer Management

D. Microsoft Management Console

220-701 A+ Objective 3.2, "Demonstrate proper use of user interfaces"

79. What Windows utility can be used to build your own customized console windows?

A. Microsoft Management Console

B. Performance Monitor

C. Computer Management

D. Services

220-701 A+ Objective 3.2, "Demonstrate proper use of user interfaces"

80. What is a single window that contains one or more administrative tools, such as Device Manager or Disk Management?

A. Clone

B. Domain

C. Workgroup

D. Console

220-701 A+ Objective 3.2, "Demonstrate proper use of user interfaces"

81. What is a useful Windows tool for troubleshooting problems with Windows, applications, and hardware?

A. Event Viewer

B. MSconfig

C. Task Manager

D. Telnet

220-701 A+ Objective 3.2, "Demonstrate proper use of user interfaces"

82. In Event Viewer, what log records events about applications and Windows utilities, such as when an application is unable to open a file or when Windows creates a restore point?

A. Security

B. System

C. Application

D. Subscription

220-701 A+ Objective 3.2, "Demonstrate proper use of user interfaces"

83. In Event Viewer, what log records events triggered by Windows components, such as a device driver failing to load during the boot process or a problem with hardware?

    A. Security

    B. System

    C. Application

    D. Subscription

    220-701 A+ Objective 3.2, "Demonstrate proper use of user interfaces"

84. In Event Viewer, what records events about installing an application?

    A. Subscription

    B. System

    C. Application

    D. Set up

    220-701 A+ Objective 3.2, "Demonstrate proper use of user interfaces"

85. In Event Viewer, what log can be customized to collect certain events you require that are not normally collected by Event Viewer?

    A. Subscription

    B. System

    C. Application

    D. Set up

    220-701 A+ Objective 3.2, "Demonstrate proper use of user interfaces"

86. Which of the following can be useful when you suspect someone is attempting to illegally log onto a system and you want to view login attempts, or when the network is giving intermittent problems?

    A. Control Panel

    B. Event Viewer

    C. Task Manager

    D. Telnet

    220-701 A+ Objective 3.2, "Demonstrate proper use of user interfaces"

87. What utility can be used to collect your own data about the system?

    A. Product activation

    B. User State Migration Tool

    C. Disk cloning

    D. Data Collector Sets

    220-701 A+ Objective 3.2, "Demonstrate proper use of user interfaces"

88. What permission allows you to write files and read existing files but does not allow you to change existing files placed in that location by others?

    A. Public

    B. Co-owner

    C. Contributor

    D. Reader

    220-701 A+ Objective 3.3, "Explain the process and steps to install and configure the Windows OS"

89. What permission allows you to have full control over the folder in the same way the owner does but is not identified as the folder owner?

    A. Public

    B. Co-owner

    C. Contributor

    D. Reader

    220-701 A+ Objective 3.3, "Explain the process and steps to install and configure the Windows OS"

90. Which of the following makes one PC (the client) appear to have a new hard drive, such as drive E, that is really a hard drive space on another host computer (the server)?

    A. Network Drive Map

    B. Kerberos

    C. CHAP

    D. BitLocker

    220-701 A+ Objective 3.3, "Explain the process and steps to install and configure the Windows OS"

91. Which of the following statements is false?

    A. A computer that does nothing but provides hard drive storage on a network for other computers is called a client computer.

    B. Mapped network drives are more reliable than using the Vista Network or XP My Network Places tool to access folders on the network.

    C. When mapping a network drive, you can type the path to the host computer rather than clicking the Browse button to navigate to the host.

    D. NFS is a type of distributed file system (DFS), which is a system that shares files on a network.

    220-701 A+ Objective 3.3, "Explain the process and steps to install and configure the Windows OS"

3

92. The Vista startup is managed by two files. One is the Windows Boot Manager (BootMgr). What is the other?

    A. Windows Vista Recovery

    B. Driver Verifier

    C. System File Checker

    D. Windows Boot Loader (WinLoad.exe)

    220-701 A+ Objective 3.4, "Explain the basics of boot sequences, methods, and startup utilities"

93. What contains the partition table and the master boot program used to locate and start the BootMgr program?

    A. System registry hive

    B. MBR

    C. BootMgr

    D. BCD

    220-701 A+ Objective 3.4, "Explain the basics of boot sequences, methods, and startup utilities"

94. What file is structured the same as a registry file and contains configuration information about how Vista is started?

    A. Recovery file

    B. Boot.ini

    C. Answer file

    D. Boot Configuration Data (BCD) file

    220-701 A+ Objective 3.4, "Explain the basics of boot sequences, methods, and startup utilities"

95. Which of the following is *not* the type of information contained in a BCD file?

    A. Settings that detect device drivers

    B. Settings that start and control the Windows Memory Diagnostic program (\Boot\MemTest.exe)

    C. Settings that launch Ntldr to load a previous OS in a dual-boot configuration

    D. Settings that control BootMgr and WinLoad.exe

    220-701 A+ Objective 3.4, "Explain the basics of boot sequences, methods, and startup utilities"

96. Which of the following boots the OS with a minimum configuration and can be used to solve problems with a new hardware installation or problems caused by user settings?

    A. Recovery console

    B. System Restore

    C. Safe Mode

    D. Emergency Repair Disk

    220-701 A+ Objective 3.4, "Explain the basics of boot sequences, methods, and startup utilities"

97. What option can be used when you are solving a problem with booting and need access to the network to solve the problem?

A. Safe Mode with Command Prompt

B. Enable VGA Mode

C. Safe Mode with Networking

D. Last Known Good Configuration

220-701 A+ Objective 3.4, "Explain the basics of boot sequences, methods, and startup utilities"

98. What are the registry settings that are saved in the registry each time the user successfully logs onto the system collectively?

A. Last Known Good Configuration

B. Boot Configuration

C. Driver Query

D. Recovery Console

220-701 A+ Objective 3.4, "Explain the basics of boot sequences, methods, and startup utilities"

99. What mode gives you the opportunity to move system boot logs from the failing computer to another computer for evaluation?

A. Last Known Good Configuration

B. Active Directory

C. Directory Services Restore Mode

D. Debugging Mode

220-701 A+ Objective 3.4, "Explain the basics of boot sequences, methods, and startup utilities"

100. Which of the following is an operating system launched from the Vista DVD that provides a graphical and command-line interface?

A. Windows Boot Loader

B. Windows Vista Recovery Environment

C. System File Checker

D. Windows Boot Manager

220-701 A+ Objective 3.4, "Explain the basics of boot sequences, methods, and startup utilities"

3

4.0

NETWORKING

1. What type of network consists of personal devices at close range such as a cell phone, PDA, and notebook computer in communication?

   A. MAN

   B. WAN

   C. LAN

   D. PAN

   220-701 A+ Objective 4.1, "Summarize the basics of networking fundamentals, including technologies, devices, and protocols"

2. What type of network covers a small local area such as a home, office, other building, or small group of buildings?

   A. PAN

   B. LAN

   C. WLAN

   D. WAN

   220-701 A+ Objective 4.1, "Summarize the basics of networking fundamentals, including technologies, devices, and protocols"

3. What type of network covers a limited geographical area and is popular where networking cables are difficult to install, such as outdoors, in public places, and in homes that are not wired for networks?

   A. PAN

   B. LAN

   C. WLAN

   D. WAN

   220-701 A+ Objective 4.1, "Summarize the basics of networking fundamentals, including technologies, devices, and protocols"

4. What is the theoretical number of bits that can be transmitted over a network at one time, similar to the number of lanes on a highway?

   A. Bandwidth

   B. ISP

   C. Data throughput

   D. Latency

   220-701 A+ Objective 4.1, "Summarize the basics of networking fundamentals, including technologies, devices, and protocols"

5. In practice, network transmissions experience delays that result in slower network performance. Which term is used to describe these delays in network transmissions?

   A. Bandwidth

   B. ISP

   C. Data throughput

   D. Latency

   220-701 A+ Objective 4.1, "Summarize the basics of networking fundamentals, including technologies, devices, and protocols"

6. Which of the following creates standards for computer and electronics industries?

   A. ANSI

   B. ISDN

   C. IEEE

   D. Ethernet

   220-701 A+ Objective 4.1, "Summarize the basics of networking fundamentals, including technologies, devices, and protocols"

7. Which term is used to describe a group of protocols that control many different aspects of communication?

   A. TCP/IP

   B. SMTP

   C. UDP

   D. ISDN

   220-701 A+ Objective 4.1, "Summarize the basics of networking fundamentals, including technologies, devices, and protocols"

8. Before data is transmitted on a network, it is broken up into which of the following?

   A. Octets

   B. Segments

   C. Subnets

   D. Switches

   220-701 A+ Objective 4.1, "Summarize the basics of networking fundamentals, including technologies, devices, and protocols"

9. Which of the following is an outdated broadband technology developed in the 1980s that uses regular phone lines and is accessed by a dial-up connection?

   A. ISDN

   B. TCP

   C. UDP

   D. SMTP

   220-701 A+ Objective 4.1, "Summarize the basics of networking fundamentals, including technologies, devices, and protocols"

10. Which statement is false?

    A. Cable modem communication uses cable lines that already exist in millions of households.

    B. With a cable modem, the TV signal to your television and the data signals to your PC share the same coax cable.

    C. Unlike cable TV, cable modems are not always connected.

    D. A cable modem converts a PC's digital signals to analog when sending them and converts incoming analog data to digital.

    220-701 A+ Objective 4.1, "Summarize the basics of networking fundamentals, including technologies, devices, and protocols"

11. Which of the following uses one upload speed from the consumer to an ISP and a faster download speed?

    A. Asymmetric DSL

    B. Cable modem

    C. Dial-up

    D. Symmetric DSL

    220-701 A+ Objective 4.1, "Summarize the basics of networking fundamentals, including technologies, devices, and protocols"

12. Which statement is false?

    A. With DSL, you share the infrastructure with your neighbors, which can result in service becoming degraded if many people in your neighborhood are using DSL at the same time.

    B. With DSL, static over phone lines in your house can be a problem.

    C. In most cases, cable modem and DSL use a network port or a USB port on the PC to connect to the cable modem or DSL box.

    D. Setup of a cable modem and DSL works about the same way, using either a cable modem box or a DSL box for the interface between the broadband jack (TV jack or phone jack) and the PC.

    220-701 A+ Objective 4.1, "Summarize the basics of networking fundamentals, including technologies, devices, and protocols"

4

13. What technology uses a dedicated line from your ISP to your place of business or residence?

    A. BNC connector

    B. Hubs

    C. Fiber optic

    D. Patch cable

    220-701 A+ Objective 4.1, "Summarize the basics of networking fundamentals, including technologies, devices, and protocols"

14. What standard(s) use(s) a frequency range of 2.4 GHz in the radio band and has (have) a distance range of about 100 meters?

    A. 802.11g and 802.11b

    B. 802.11n

    C. 802.11a

    D. 802.11k and 802.11r

    220-701 A+ Objective 4.1, "Summarize the basics of networking fundamentals, including technologies, devices, and protocols"

15. What standard(s) use(s) multiple input/multiple output (MIMO) technology, whereby two or more antennas are used at both ends of transmission?

    A. 802.11g and 802.11b

    B. 802.11n

    C. 802.11a

    D. 802.11k and 802.11r

    220-701 A+ Objective 4.1, "Summarize the basics of networking fundamentals, including technologies, devices, and protocols"

16. Which statement is false?

    A. 802.11g runs at 54 Mbps and 802.11b runs at 11 Mbps.

    B. 802.11n can use the 2.4-GHz range and be compatible with 802.11b/g.

    C. 802.11b/g has the disadvantage that many cordless phones use the 2.4-GHz frequency range and cause network interference.

    D. The 802.11r standard defines how wireless network traffic can better be distributed over multiple access points covering a wide area so that the access point with the strongest signal is not overloaded.

    220-701 A+ Objective 4.1, "Summarize the basics of networking fundamentals, including technologies, devices, and protocols"

17. Which statement is false?

    A. WEP encryption is considered secure.

    B. WPA encryption, also called TKIP (Temporal Key Integrity Protocol) encryption, is stronger than WEP and was designed to replace it.

    C. WEP was first defined by 802.11b.

    D. With WEP encryption, data is encrypted using either 64-bit or 128-bit encryption keys.

    220-701 A+ Objective 4.3, "Compare and contrast the different network types"

18. What is a 6-byte number that uniquely identifies a network adapter on a computer?

A. IP address

B. Access point

C. MAC address

D. Port address

220-701 A+ Objective 4.3, "Compare and contrast the different network types"

19. Which of the following supports up to 75 Mbps with a range up to several miles and uses 2- to 11-GHz frequency?

A. WiMAX

B. SSID

C. WEP

D. WPA

220-701 A+ Objective 4.3, "Compare and contrast the different network types"

20. Which term is used to describe an open standard that uses digital communication of data and is accepted and used worldwide?

A. GSM

B. CDMA

C. TDMA

D. WPA

220-701 A+ Objective 4.3, "Compare and contrast the different network types"

21. What is a standard for short-range wireless communication and data synchronization between devices?

A. WPA

B. TDMA

C. Bluetooth

D. GSM

220-701 A+ Objective 4.3, "Compare and contrast the different network types"

22. Which of the following is known as a line protocol?

A. DHCP

B. CAT-3

C. CAT-5

D. PPP

220-701 A+ Objective 4.3, "Compare and contrast the different network types"

23. Which statement is false?

    A. Laptops can make connections to a network through a PC Card NIC, a built-in network port, or an external device that connects to the laptop by way of a USB port.

    B. For a network port on the motherboard, a solid light indicates activity and a blinking light indicates connectivity.

    C. A desktop-to-laptop computer connects to a local network using an Ethernet wired network or wireless networking.

    D. Most network cards provide status light indicators near the RJ-45 port.

    220-701 A+ Objective 4.1, "Summarize the basics of networking fundamentals, including technologies, devices, and protocols"

24. Which statement is false?

    A. No two adapters should have the same MAC address.

    B. Every NIC used today for a wired network follows the Ethernet standards.

    C. The four speeds for Ethernet are 5 Mbps, 10 Mbps (Fast Ethernet), 1 Gbps (Gigabit Ethernet), and 5 Gbps (10-gigabit Ethernet).

    D. An example of a MAC address is 00-0C-6E-4E-AB-A5.

    220-701 A+ Objective 4.1, "Summarize the basics of networking fundamentals, including technologies, devices, and protocols"

25. Which statement is false?

    A. Twisted-pair cable comes in two varieties: unshielded twisted pair (UTP) cable and shielded twisted pair (STP) cable.

    B. STP uses a covering around the pairs of wires inside the cable that protects it from electromagnetic interference caused by electrical motors, transmitters, or high-tension lines.

    C. CAT-6 has more crosstalk than CAT-5 or CAT-5e.

    D. Twisted-pair cable is the most popular cabling method for local networks.

    220-701 A+ Objective 4.2, "Categorize network cables and connectors and their implementations"

26. Which of the following has a single copper wire down the middle and a braided shield around it?

    A. Coaxial cable

    B. Twisted-pair cable

    C. Fiber-optic cable

    D. Shielded twisted pair

    220-701 A+ Objective 4.2, "Categorize network cables and connectors and their implementations"

27. Which of the following transmits signals as pulses of light over glass strands inside protected tubing?

    A. Coaxial cable

    B. Twisted-pair cable

    C. Fiber-optic cable

    D. Shielded twisted pair

    220-701 A+ Objective 4.2, "Categorize network cables and connectors and their implementations"

28. What type of cable uses a single path for light to travel in the cable?

    A. Coaxial cable

    B. Twisted-pair cable

    C. Single-mode cable

    D. Multimode fiber-optic cable

    220-701 A+ Objective 4.2, "Categorize network cables and connectors and their implementations"

29. What is currently replacing 100BaseT Ethernet as the choice for LAN technology?

    A. GSM

    B. Gigabit Ethernet

    C. Bluetooth

    D. CDMA

    220-701 A+ Objective 4.2, "Categorize network cables and connectors and their implementations"

30. What is thought of as just a pass-through and distribution point for every device connected to it, without regard for what kind of data is passing through and where the data might be going?

    A. Hub

    B. Switch

    C. Segment

    D. Port

    220-701 A+ Objective 4.1, "Summarize the basics of networking fundamentals, including technologies, devices, and protocols"

31. What keeps a table of all the devices connected to it and uses this table to determine which path to use when sending packets?

    A. Segment

    B. Port

    C. Hub

    D. Switch

    220-701 A+ Objective 4.1, "Summarize the basics of networking fundamentals, including technologies, devices, and protocols"

32. What name describes a type of cable that connects a computer to a hub or switch?

    A. Crossover cable

    B. Fiber optic

    C. Patch cable

    D. Cellular WAN

    220-701 A+ Objective 4.1, "Summarize the basics of networking fundamentals, including technologies, devices, and protocols"

33. What name describes a type of cable that connects two like devices such as a switch to a switch or a PC to a PC (to make the simplest network of all)?

    A. Crossover cable

    B. Cellular WAN

    C. Patch cable

    D. 10BaseT

    220-701 A+ Objective 4.1, "Summarize the basics of networking fundamentals, including technologies, devices, and protocols"

34. What name describes a device that manages traffic between two networks?

    A. Switch

    B. Port

    C. Hub

    D. Router

    220-701 A+ Objective 4.1, "Summarize the basics of networking fundamentals, including technologies, devices, and protocols"

35. What name describes a server that gives IP addresses to computers on the network when they attempt to initiate a connection to the network and request an IP address?

    A. TCP/IP

    B. Dynamic host configuration protocol

    C. Bluetooth

    D. Network Address Translation

    220-701 A+ Objective 4.1, "Summarize the basics of networking fundamentals, including technologies, devices, and protocols"

36. Which term describes a protocol that substitutes the IP address of the router for the IP address of other computers inside the network when these computers need to communicate on the Internet?

    A. Network Address Translation

    B. Dynamic Host Configuration Protocol

    C. Firewall

    D. TCP/IP

    220-701 A+ Objective 4.1, "Summarize the basics of networking fundamentals, including technologies, devices, and protocols"

37. Which of the following is described as being at the root level of communication?

    A. Software

    B. Operating system

    C. Hardware

    D. NIC

    220-701 A+ Objective 4.1, "Summarize the basics of networking fundamentals, including technologies, devices, and protocols"

38. Which of the following is responsible for managing communication between itself and another computer, using rules for communication that both operating systems understand?

    A. Software

    B. Operating system

    C. Hardware

    D. NIC

    220-701 A+ Objective 4.1, "Summarize the basics of networking fundamentals, including technologies, devices, and protocols"

39. What is a 32-bit string used to identify a computer on a network?

    A. IP address

    B. NAT

    C. Router

    D. NIC

    220-701 A+ Objective 4.1, "Summarize the basics of networking fundamentals, including technologies, devices, and protocols"

40. Which of the following terms refers to a situation in which each computer on a network is assigned an IP address that never changes?

    A. Static IP addressing

    B. Network Address Translation

    C. Multicasting

    D. Dynamic IP addressing

    220-701 A+ Objective 4.1, "Summarize the basics of networking fundamentals, including technologies, devices, and protocols"

41. Which of the following terms refers to a situation in which each time the computer connects to the network, it gets a new IP address from the DHCP server?

    A. Static IP addressing

    B. Multicasting

    C. Dynamic IP addressing

    D. Network Address Translation

    220-701 A+ Objective 4.1, "Summarize the basics of networking fundamentals, including technologies, devices, and protocols"

42. When you use the Internet to surf the Web or download your e-mail, you are, in fact, using an application on your computer. What is this application called?

    A. Extranet

    B. Internet client

    C. Socket

    D. Intranet

    220-701 A+ Objective 4.1, "Summarize the basics of networking fundamentals, including technologies, devices, and protocols"

43. You can address a Web server by entering into a browser address box an IP address followed by a colon and then the port number. What are these values known as?

    A. Segments

    B. Internet clients

    C. Packets

    D. Sockets

    220-701 A+ Objective 4.1, "Summarize the basics of networking fundamentals, including technologies, devices, and protocols"

44. Which of the following is a private network that uses TCP/IP protocols?

    A. Intranet

    B. Internet

    C. Bluetooth

    D. DHCP

    220-701 A+ Objective 4.1, "Summarize the basics of networking fundamentals, including technologies, devices, and protocols"

45. What is the largest possible 8-bit number?

    A. 11111111

    B. 10110111

    C. 10110100

    D. 10110110

    220-701 A+ Objective 4.1, "Summarize the basics of networking fundamentals, including technologies, devices, and protocols"

46. The first part of an IP address identifies which of the following?

    A. Port

    B. Host

    C. Network

    D. Packet

    220-701 A+ Objective 4.1, "Summarize the basics of networking fundamentals, including technologies, devices, and protocols"

47. Who is responsible for keeping track of assigned IP addresses and domain names?

A. DHCP

B. ICANN

C. IEEE

D. ANSI

220-701 A+ Objective 4.1, "Summarize the basics of networking fundamentals, including technologies, devices, and protocols"

48. Class D addresses begin with octets 224 through 239 and are used for which of the following?

A. Multicasting

B. NAT

C. SMTP authentication

D. Data throughput

220-701 A+ Objective 4.1, "Summarize the basics of networking fundamentals, including technologies, devices, and protocols"

49. Class E addresses begin with 240 through 254 and are reserved for which of the following?

A. Multicasting

B. Ports

C. Research

D. Name resolution

220-701 A+ Objective 4.1, "Summarize the basics of networking fundamentals, including technologies, devices, and protocols"

50. What is used in the TCP/IP configuration for a network and tells the OS which part of an IP address is the network portion and which part identifies the host?

A. UDP

B. Thicknet

C. Hub

D. Subnet mask

220-701 A+ Objective 4.1, "Summarize the basics of networking fundamentals, including technologies, devices, and protocols"

51. What name describes subnet masks that contain all 1s or all 0s in an octet?

A. ThinNet

B. Classful

C. Switch

D. Router

220-701 A+ Objective 4.1, "Summarize the basics of networking fundamentals, including technologies, devices, and protocols"

4

52. Which term describes IP addresses available to the Internet?

   A. Subnet masks

   B. Private IP addresses

   C. Routers

   D. Public IP addresses

   220-701 A+ Objective 4.1, "Summarize the basics of networking fundamentals, including technologies, devices, and protocols"

53. Which of the following is used on private intranets that are not allowed on the Internet?

   A. Subnet masks

   B. Private IP addresses

   C. Routers

   D. Public IP addresses

   220-701 A+ Objective 4.1, "Summarize the basics of networking fundamentals, including technologies, devices, and protocols"

54. Which statement is false?

   A. All IP addresses on a network must be unique for that network.

   B. When a workstation has an IP address assigned to it, it is said that the workstation is borrowing the IP address.

   C. An ISP customarily uses dynamic IP addressing for its individual subscribers.

   D. DHCP software resides on both the client and the server to manage the dynamic assignments of IP addresses.

   220-701 A+ Objective 4.1, "Summarize the basics of networking fundamentals, including technologies, devices, and protocols"

55. What is a computer name that can be used in place of its IP address?

   A. DNS

   B. NetBIOS

   C. Host name

   D. FQDN

   220-701 A+ Objective 4.1, "Summarize the basics of networking fundamentals, including technologies, devices, and protocols"

56. What protocol is used by applications to communicate with each other?

   A. UDP

   B. NetBIOS

   C. Bluetooth

   D. Fully qualified domain name

   220-701 A+ Objective 4.1, "Summarize the basics of networking fundamentals, including technologies, devices, and protocols"

57. What identifies a computer and the network to which it belongs?

A. Fully qualified domain name

B. NetBIOS

C. UDP

D. DNS

220-701 A+ Objective 4.1, "Summarize the basics of networking fundamentals, including technologies, devices, and protocols"

58. What name is given to the process of associating a character-based name with an IP address?

A. Network Address Translation

B. IP addressing

C. Name resolution

D. Multicasting

220-701 A+ Objective 4.1, "Summarize the basics of networking fundamentals, including technologies, devices, and protocols"

59. What device can find an IP address for a computer when the fully qualified domain name is known?

A. Hub

B. DNS server

C. Switch

D. Port

220-701 A+ Objective 4.1, "Summarize the basics of networking fundamentals, including technologies, devices, and protocols"

60. Where should Windows look first when trying to resolve a computer name to an IP address?

A. Router

B. DNS server

C. Packet

D. Hosts file

220-701 A+ Objective 4.1, "Summarize the basics of networking fundamentals, including technologies, devices, and protocols"

61. What World Wide Web protocol is used by Web browsers and Web servers to communicate?

A. HTTP

B. FTP

C. UDP

D. SMTP

220-701 A+ Objective 4.1, "Summarize the basics of networking fundamentals, including technologies, devices, and protocols"

4

62. What protocol is used by Web browsers and servers to encrypt the data before it is sent and then decrypt it before the data is processed?

    A. FTP

    B. UDP

    C. HTTPS

    D. SMTP

    220-701 A+ Objective 4.1, "Summarize the basics of networking fundamentals, including technologies, devices, and protocols"

63. What protocol is used to transfer files between two computers?

    A. FTP

    B. SMTP

    C. HTTPS

    D. UDP

    220-701 A+ Objective 4.1, "Summarize the basics of networking fundamentals, including technologies, devices, and protocols"

64. What protocol is used to authenticate a user to an e-mail server when the e-mail client first tries to connect to the e-mail server to send e-mail?

    A. FTP

    B. SMTP

    C. HTTPS

    D. SMTP AUTH

    220-701 A+ Objective 4.1, "Summarize the basics of networking fundamentals, including technologies, devices, and protocols"

65. What protocol is used by client/server applications to allow an administrator or other user to control a computer remotely?

    A. FTP

    B. SMTP

    C. Telnet

    D. SMTP AUTH

    220-701 A+ Objective 4.1, "Summarize the basics of networking fundamentals, including technologies, devices, and protocols"

66. In TCP/IP, what name is used to describe the protocol that guarantees packet delivery?

    A. FTP

    B. TCP

    C. Telnet

    D. UDP

    220-701 A+ Objective 4.1, "Summarize the basics of networking fundamentals, including technologies, devices, and protocols"

67. Which of the following is a connectionless protocol (also called a best-effort protocol)?

    A. FTP

    B. TCP

    C. Telnet

    D. UDP

    220-701 A+ Objective 4.1, "Summarize the basics of networking fundamentals, including technologies, devices, and protocols"

68. What command tests connectivity by sending an echo request to a remote computer?

    A. Ping

    B. TCP

    C. Telnet

    D. Ipconfig

    220-701 A+ Objective 4.1, "Summarize the basics of networking fundamentals, including technologies, devices, and protocols"

4

69. What command can display TCP/IP configuration information and refresh the IP address?

    A. Ping

    B. TCP

    C. Telnet

    D. Ipconfig

    220-701 A+ Objective 4.1, "Summarize the basics of networking fundamentals, including technologies, devices, and protocols"

70. What Telnet command displays command responses that are given by the remote computer?

    A. Set ntlm

    B. Set localecho

    C. Open <host name> [port]

    D. Ctrl+]

    220-701 A+ Objective 4.1, "Summarize the basics of networking fundamentals, including technologies, devices, and protocols"

71. What Telnet command switches from the remote computer session mode window to the Telnet command mode window?

    A. Set ntlm

    B. Set localecho

    C. Open <host name> [port]

    D. Ctrl+]

    220-701 A+ Objective 4.1, "Summarize the basics of networking fundamentals, including technologies, devices, and protocols"

72. Which of the following works by using encrypted data packets between a private network and a computer somewhere on the Internet?

   A. VPN

   B. Intranet

   C. Extranet

   D. WAN

   220-701 A+ Objective 4.1, "Summarize the basics of networking fundamentals, including technologies, devices, and protocols"

73. What is a group of four dotted decimal numbers, such as 255.255.0.0, that tells TCP/IP if a computer's IP address is on the same or a different network?

   A. Gateway

   B. Port

   C. Subnet mask

   D. Router

   220-701 A+ Objective 4.1, "Summarize the basics of networking fundamentals, including technologies, devices, and protocols"

74. What is a computer or other device, such as a router, that allows a computer on one network to communicate with a computer on another network?

   A. Gateway

   B. Port

   C. Subnet mask

   D. Hub

   220-701 A+ Objective 4.1, "Summarize the basics of networking fundamentals, including technologies, devices, and protocols"

75. Which of the following is the gateway a computer uses to access another network if it does not have a better option?

   A. Default gateway

   B. Port

   C. Subnet mask

   D. Bluetooth

   220-701 A+ Objective 4.1, "Summarize the basics of networking fundamentals, including technologies, devices, and protocols"

5.0

SECURITY

1. Which of the following includes regulations to secure patient data that applies to all health care companies and professionals?

   A. IEEE

   B. ISO

   C. NIST

   D. HIPAA

   220-701 A+ Objective 5.1, "Explain the basic principles of security concepts and technologies"

2. Which of the following has published information technology standards for security to be followed by the U.S. government and its contractors?

   A. IEEE

   B. ISO

   C. NIST

   D. HIPAA

   220-701 A+ Objective 5.1, "Explain the basic principles of security concepts and technologies"

3. Which statement is false?

   A. Your first steps to making a security plan are to find out what standards, if any, your employer or company must follow.

   B. The security plan need not change with the organization.

   C. Implement each security method you decide to use.

   D. A security plan needs to include methods to monitor the security of a system.

   220-701 A+ Objective 5.1, "Explain the basic principles of security concepts and technologies"

4. What proves that an individual is who he says he is and is accomplished by a variety of techniques, including a username, password, and personal identification number?

   A. Authorization

   B. Encryption

   C. Social engineering

   D. Authentication

   220-701 A+ Objective 5.1, "Explain the basic principles of security concepts and technologies"

5. What determines what an individual can do in the system after he is authenticated?

   A. Authorization

   B. Encryption

   C. Social engineering

   D. Classification

   220-701 A+ Objective 5.1, "Explain the basic principles of security concepts and technologies"

6. Because of the problem of losing encrypted data and Internet passwords when a user password is reset, what should each new user create for use in the event that he forgets the password?

   A. Guest account

   B. Password reset disk

   C. Rootkit

   D. Power user account

   220-701 A+ Objective 5.1, "Explain the basic principles of security concepts and technologies"

7. Power-on passwords are assigned in BIOS setup. Where in the computer are they kept to prevent unauthorized access to the computer or to the BIOS setup utility?

   A. CMOS RAM

   B. Registry

   C. Microprocessor

   D. Main board

   220-701 A+ Objective 5.1, "Explain the basic principles of security concepts and technologies"

8. Some notebooks give you the option of setting a hard drive password, which is set in BIOS setup and written on the hard drive. What is the name given to this type of password?

   A. Power-on passwords

   B. Kerberos

   C. Drive lock password

   D. CHAP

   220-701 A+ Objective 5.1, "Explain the basic principles of security concepts and technologies"

9. Which term describes the protocols that are used to encrypt account names and passwords?

   A. Drive lock protocols

   B. BIOS protocols

   C. Authorization protocols

   D. Authentication protocols

   220-701 A+ Objective 5.1, "Explain the basic principles of security concepts and technologies"

10. Which of the following is the default protocol used by Windows Vista/XP?

    A. CHAP

    B. EFS

    C. Kerberos

    D. Rootkit

    220-701 A+ Objective 5.1, "Explain the basic principles of security concepts and technologies"

11. What is the term to describe any small device that contains authentication information that can be keyed into a logon window by a user?

    A. BitLocker

    B. CHAP

    C. Kerberos

    D. Smart card

    220-701 A+ Objective 5.1, "Explain the basic principles of security concepts and technologies"

12. What is assigned by a Certification Authority and is used to prove you are who you say you are?

    A. Digital certificate

    B. Smart card

    C. VPN

    D. Rootkit

    220-701 A+ Objective 5.1, "Explain the basic principles of security concepts and technologies"

13. What is designed to help encrypt any data sent over the Internet to the corporate network, such as that used by a VPN?

    A. Digital certificate

    B. Smart card

    C. Rootkit

    D. Biometric device

    220-701 A+ Objective 5.1, "Explain the basic principles of security concepts and technologies"

14. Which term describes a device that inputs biological data about a person, where the data can identify a person's fingerprints, handprints, face, voice, eye, and handwritten signatures?

    A. Digital certificate

    B. Biometric device

    C. Key fob

    D. Key logger

    220-701 A+ Objective 5.1, "Explain the basic principles of security concepts and technologies"

5

15. What word would you use to describe a password that is not easy to guess by humans and computer programs designed to hack passwords?

    A. Unique password

    B. Smart password

    C. Passphrase

    D. Strong password

    220-701 A+ Objective 5.1, "Explain the basic principles of security concepts and technologies"

16. What is made of several words, with spaces allowed?

    A. Key logger

    B. Digital Certificate

    C. Passphrase

    D. Password

    220-701 A+ Objective 5.1, "Explain the basic principles of security concepts and technologies"

17. Which of the following does *not* meet the criteria of a strong password?

    A. Use at least one symbol in the second through sixth position of your password.

    B. Combine uppercase and lowercase letters, numbers, and symbols.

    C. Use consecutive letters or numbers, such as "abcdefg" or "12345."

    D. Use eight or more characters (14 characters or longer is better).

    220-701 A+ Objective 5.1, "Explain the basic principles of security concepts and technologies"

18. Which Vista account has complete access to the system and can make changes that affect the security of the system and other users?

    A. Administrator account

    B. Guest account

    C. Standard account

    D. Limited account

    220-701 A+ Objective 5.1, "Explain the basic principles of security concepts and technologies"

19. Which Vista account can use software and hardware and make some system changes but cannot make changes that affect the security of the system or other users?

    A. Administrator account

    B. Guest account

    C. Standard account

    D. Limited account

    220-701 A+ Objective 5.1, "Explain the basic principles of security concepts and technologies"

20. Which Vista account is not normally activated and has limited rights?

    A. Guest account

    B. Standard account

    C. Limited account

    D. Administrative account

    220-701 A+ Objective 5.1, "Explain the basic principles of security concepts and technologies"

21. Which Vista account has read-write access only on its own folders, read-only access to most system folders, and no access to other users' data?

   A. Guest account

   B. Standard account

   C. Limited account

   D. Administrative account

   220-701 A+ Objective 5.1, "Explain the basic principles of security concepts and technologies"

22. Which of the following involves putting data into categories and then deciding how secure each category must be?

   A. Permissions

   B. Data classification

   C. Encryption

   D. Social engineering

   220-701 A+ Objective 5.1, "Explain the basic principles of security concepts and technologies"

23. What type of encryption works only when using Windows NTFS, the Windows Vista Ultimate and Business editions, and Windows XP Professional?

   A. Encrypted File System

   B. CHAP

   C. Trusted Platform Module

   D. Public-Key Infrastructure

   220-701 A+ Objective 5.1, "Explain the basic principles of security concepts and technologies"

24. In Windows Vista Ultimate and Enterprise editions, what locks down a hard drive by encrypting the entire Vista volume and any other volume on the drive?

   A. Rootkits

   B. Smart cards

   C. Digital certificates

   D. BitLocker encryption

   220-701 A+ Objective 5.1, "Explain the basic principles of security concepts and technologies"

25. Digital certificates are transported over the Internet and verified using which of the following standards?

   A. Public-Key Infrastructure

   B. VPN

   C. Encrypted File System

   D. Kerberos

   220-701 A+ Objective 5.1, "Explain the basic principles of security concepts and technologies"

5

26. What name is given to the chip on the motherboard of many high-end computers?

    A. Trojan horse

    B. Grayware

    C. Trusted Platform Module chip

    D. Rootkit

    220-701 A+ Objective 5.2, "Summarize the following security features"

27. To keep a system secure, users need to practice the habit of locking down their workstation each time they step away from their desks. What is the quickest way to do this?

    A. Press the Ctrl key and M

    B. Press the Alt key and L

    C. Press the Shift key and R

    D. Press the Windows key and L

    220-701 A+ Objective 5.2, "Summarize the following security features"

28. Which term describes an unwanted program that intends to harm you and is transmitted to your computer without your knowledge?

    A. Malicious software

    B. BitLocker Encryption

    C. Macro

    D. Backdoor

    220-701 A+ Objective 5.2, "Summarize the following security features"

29. What name is given to any annoying and unwanted program that may or may not intend to harm you?

    A. Adware

    B. Malware

    C. Grayware

    D. Worm

    220-701 A+ Objective 5.2, "Summarize the following security features"

30. What name is given to a program that replicates by attaching itself to other programs?

    A. Adware

    B. Virus

    C. Hijacker

    D. Spyware

    220-701 A+ Objective 5.2, "Summarize the following security features"

31. Which of the following is secretly installed on your computer when you download and install shareware or freeware, including screen savers, desktop wallpaper, music, cartoons, news, and weather alerts?

    A. Rootkit

    B. BitLocker Encryption

    C. Adware

    D. PKI

    220-701 A+ Objective 5.2, "Summarize the following security features"

32. Which term describes software that installs itself on your computer to spy on you and to collect personal information about you?

    A. Spyware

    B. Virus

    C. Adware

    D. Worm

    220-701 A+ Objective 5.2, "Summarize the following security features"

33. Which of the following tracks all your keystrokes, including passwords, chat room sessions, e-mail messages, documents, online purchases, and anything else you type on your PC?

    A. Spyware

    B. Keylogger

    C. Adware

    D. Rootkit

    220-701 A+ Objective 5.2, "Summarize the following security features"

34. Which term describes a program that copies itself throughout a network or the Internet without a host program?

    A. Worm

    B. Keylogger

    C. Adware

    D. Browser hijacker

    220-701 A+ Objective 5.2, "Summarize the following security features"

35. Which term describes junk e-mail that you do not want, you did not ask for, and that gets in your way?

    A. Worm

    B. Keylogger

    C. Adware

    D. Spam

    220-701 A+ Objective 5.2, "Summarize the following security features"

5

36. Which of the following is a type of identity theft where the sender of an e-mail message scams you into responding with personal data about yourself?

    A. Worm

    B. Keylogger

    C. Phishing

    D. Spam

    220-701 A+ Objective 5.2, "Summarize the following security features"

37. Which term describes dormant code added to software and triggered at a predetermined time or by a predetermined event?

    A. Logic bomb

    B. Keylogger

    C. Phishing

    D. Spam

    220-701 A+ Objective 5.2, "Summarize the following security features"

38. Which of the following can hide in either of two boot sectors of a hard drive?

    A. Logic bomb

    B. Macro

    C. Rootkit

    D. Boot sector virus

    220-701 A+ Objective 5.2, "Summarize the following security features"

39. Which term describes a small program contained in a document that can be automatically executed either when the document is first loaded or later by pressing a key combination?

    A. Logic bomb

    B. Macro

    C. Trojan Horse

    D. Boot sector virus

    220-701 A+ Objective 5.2, "Summarize the following security features"

40. What is known in the computer arena as the practice of tricking people into giving out private information or allowing unsafe programs into the network or computer?

    A. Social engineering

    B. Macro

    C. Phishing

    D. Encryption

    220-701 A+ Objective 5.2, "Summarize the following security features"

6.0

OPERATIONAL PROCEDURE

1. Which of the following explains how to properly handle substances such as chemical solvents?

   A. Trip hazard

   B. Material Safety Data Sheet

   C. Site license

   D. Rootkit

   220-701 A+ Objective 6.1, "Outline the purpose of appropriate safety and environmental procedures and given a scenario apply them"

2. Which of the following includes information such as physical data, toxicity, health effects, first aid, storage, shipping, disposal, and spill procedures?

   A. Trip hazard

   B. Site license

   C. Rootkit

   D. MSDS

   220-701 A+ Objective 6.1, "Outline the purpose of appropriate safety and environmental procedures and given a scenario apply them"

3. How should you dispose of alkaline batteries, including AAA, AA, A, C, D, and 9-volt?

   A. Dispose of these batteries in the regular trash.

   B. Dispose of them by returning them to the original dealer or by taking them to a recycling center.

   C. Return them to the manufacturer or dealer to be recycled.

   D. Consider using a data-destruction service.

   220-701 A+ Objective 6.1, "Outline the purpose of appropriate safety and environmental procedures and given a scenario apply them"

6

4. How should you dispose of button batteries used in digital cameras and other small equipment, such as battery packs used in notebooks?

   A. Dispose of these batteries in the regular trash.

   B. Dispose of them by returning them to the original dealer or by taking them to a recycling center.

   C. Check with local county or environmental officials for laws and regulations in your area for proper disposal of these items.

   D. Consider using a data-destruction service.

   220-701 A+ Objective 6.1, "Outline the purpose of appropriate safety and environmental procedures and given a scenario apply them"

5. When preparing a computer for shipping, which of the following would you *not* want to do?

   A. Back up all important data on the computer.

   B. Coil all external cords and secure them with plastic ties or rubber bands.

   C. Pack the computer, monitor, and all devices in their original shipping cartons or similar boxes with enough packing material to protect them.

   D. Refuse insurance on the shipment.

   220-701 A+ Objective 6.1, "Outline the purpose of appropriate safety and environmental procedures and given a scenario apply them"

6. What trait positively distinguishes one competent technician from another in the eyes of the customer?

   A. An assertive attitude

   B. Minimizing the problem

   C. Talking to coworkers on the job

   D. Proper and polite language

   220-701 A+ Objective 6.1, "Outline the purpose of appropriate safety and environmental procedures and given a scenario apply them"

7. When preparing for an on-site service call, which of the following is *not* recommended?

   A. Know the problem you are going to address.

   B. Know the urgency of the situation.

   C. Know what computer, software, and hardware needs servicing.

   D. Concentrate on technical skills and ignore interpersonal skills.

   220-701 A+ Objective 6.2, "Given a scenario, demonstrate the appropriate use of communication skills and professionalism in the workplace"

8. When working at a user's desk, which of the following should you *not* do?

   A. Ask permission before using the printer or other equipment.

   B. Feel free to use the phone as needed.

   C. Accept personal inconvenience to accommodate the user's urgent business needs.

   D. If the user is present, ask permission before you make a software or hardware change, even if the user has just given you permission to interact with the PC.

   220-701 A+ Objective 6.2, "Given a scenario, demonstrate the appropriate use of communication skills and professionalism in the workplace"

9. As a support technician, which of the following is *not* advisable when interviewing a customer?

   A. Ask him to listen while you repeat the problem to make sure you understand it correctly.

   B. If you do not understand what the customer is telling you, ask open-ended questions to try to narrow down the specifics of the problem.

   C. Always make assumptions.

   D. Use diplomacy and good manners.

   220-701 A+ Objective 6.2, "Given a scenario, demonstrate the appropriate use of communication skills and professionalism in the workplace"

10. How does troubleshooting begin?

    A. By moving the computer

    B. By installing software

    C. By disconnecting the computer

    D. By interviewing the user

    220-701 A+ Objective 6.2, "Given a scenario, demonstrate the appropriate use of communication skills and professionalism in the workplace"

11. When conducting an interview, which of the following questions is least likely to help you learn as much as you can about the problem?

    A. Did you drop the PC?

    B. Please describe the problem. What error messages, unusual displays, or failures did you see?

    C. When did the problem start?

    D. What was the situation when the problem occurred?

    220-701 A+ Objective 6.2, "Given a scenario, demonstrate the appropriate use of communication skills and professionalism in the workplace"

12. While working with a customer on the phone, which of the following would you consider inappropriate?

    A. If your call is accidentally disconnected, call back immediately.

    B. Complain about your job, your boss or coworkers, your company, or other companies or products to your customers.

    C. Speak clearly and don't talk too fast.

    D. If you must put callers on hold, tell them how long it will be before you get back to them.

    220-701 A+ Objective 6.2, "Given a scenario, demonstrate the appropriate use of communication skills and professionalism in the workplace"

6

13. Which of the following is the most difficult situation to handle when a customer is not knowledgeable about how to use a computer?

   A. Help desk call

   B. On-site visit

   C. Listening

   D. Working with coworkers

   220-701 A+ Objective 6.2, "Given a scenario, demonstrate the appropriate use of communication skills and professionalism in the workplace"

14. Which of the following suggestions will *not* help you handle complaints and defuse customer anger?

   A. Being an active listener and letting customers know they are not being ignored.

   B. Giving the customer a little time to vent and apologizing when you can.

   C. Defending your company's position until the customer is in agreement.

   D. Knowing how your employer wants you to handle a situation where you are verbally abused.

   220-701 A+ Objective 6.2, "Given a scenario, demonstrate the appropriate use of communication skills and professionalism in the workplace"

15. For on-site work, after you have solved the problem, which of the following tasks would you be least likely to do before closing the call?

   A. If you changed anything on the PC after you booted it, reboot one more time to make sure you have not caused a problem with the boot.

   B. Inform the customer that after you leave, she should check that the printer is still working and that the network is still connected.

   C. If you backed up data before working on the problem and then restored the data from backups, ask the user to verify that the data is fully restored.

   D. Explain preventive maintenance to the customer.

   220-701 A+ Objective 6.2, "Given a scenario, demonstrate the appropriate use of communication skills and professionalism in the workplace"

16. Which statement is false?

   A. A surge suppressor might be a series type that blocks the surge from flowing.

   B. A surge suppressor might be a shunt type that absorbs the surge.

   C. All power strips are surge suppressors.

   D. Some power strips only multiply the number of outlets without offering protection from a power surge.

   220-701 A+ Objective 6.1, "Outline the purpose of appropriate safety and environmental procedures and given a scenario apply them"

17. When providing on-site support, what does the customer expect the most?

    A. A new computer

    B. Free samples

    C. Polite conversation

    D. Documentation about your services

    220-701 A+ Objective 6.2, "Given a scenario, demonstrate the appropriate use of communication skills and professionalism in the workplace"

18. What name is given to someone who puts business matters above personal matters?

    A. Organizer

    B. Professional

    C. Coworker

    D. Client

    220-701 A+ Objective 6.2, "Given a scenario, demonstrate the appropriate use of communication skills and professionalism in the workplace"

19. Which of the following holds its charge even after the power is turned off and the device is unplugged?

    A. Capacitor

    B. Conductor

    C. Field replaceable unit

    D. Ground

    220-701 A+ Objective 6.1, "Outline the purpose of appropriate safety and environmental procedures and given a scenario apply them"

20. What is the easiest possible path for electricity to follow?

    A. Capacitor

    B. Conductor

    C. Ground

    D. Field replaceable unit

    220-701 A+ Objective 6.1, "Outline the purpose of appropriate safety and environmental procedures and given a scenario apply them"

21. Which term is used to describe the power supply and monitor?

    A. Capacitor

    B. Field replaceable unit

    C. Conductor

    D. Ground

    220-701 A+ Objective 6.1, "Outline the purpose of appropriate safety and environmental procedures and given a scenario apply them"

6

22. Which term is used to describe an electrical charge at rest?

    A. Static electricity

    B. Field replaceable unit

    C. Capacity

    D. Underground conductor

    220-701 A+ Objective 6.1, "Outline the purpose of appropriate safety and environmental procedures and given a scenario apply them"

23. Which of the following holds a charge until the charge is released?

    A. Riser card

    B. Form factor

    C. Ungrounded conductor

    D. Smart UPS

    220-701 A+ Objective 6.1, "Outline the purpose of appropriate safety and environmental procedures and given a scenario apply them"

24. Which statement is false?

    A. When two objects with dissimilar electrical charges touch, electricity passes between them until the dissimilar charges become equal.

    B. A charge of only 10 volts can damage electronic components.

    C. ESD can cause two types of damage in an electronic component: catastrophic failure and upset failure.

    D. A catastrophic failure damages the component so that it does not perform well, even though it may still function to some degree.

    220-701 A+ Objective 6.1, "Outline the purpose of appropriate safety and environmental procedures and given a scenario apply them"

25. What contains a resistor that prevents electricity from harming you?

    A. Ground bracelet

    B. Riser card

    C. Transistor

    D. Diode

    220-701 A+ Objective 6.1, "Outline the purpose of appropriate safety and environmental procedures and given a scenario apply them"

26. What dissipates ESD and is commonly used by bench technicians (also called depot technicians) who repair and assemble computers at their workbenches or in an assembly line?

    A. Ground bracelet

    B. Ground mat

    C. Static shielding bag

    D. Diode

    220-701 A+ Objective 6.1, "Outline the purpose of appropriate safety and environmental procedures and given a scenario apply them"

27. What name is given to a device that protects against an electromagnetic field?

    A. Resistor

    B. Multimeter

    C. Bus riser

    D. Faraday cage

    220-701 A+ Objective 6.1, "Outline the purpose of appropriate safety and environmental procedures and given a scenario apply them"

28. Which of the following is designed to prevent an ESD between you and a device as you pick it up and handle it?

    A. Ground bracelet

    B. Antistatic gloves

    C. Ground mat

    D. Faraday cage

    220-701 A+ Objective 6.1, "Outline the purpose of appropriate safety and environmental procedures and given a scenario apply them"

29. What is caused by the magnetic field produced as a side effect when electricity flows?

    A. Electromagnetic interference

    B. ATX

    C. Brownout

    D. Joule

    220-701 A+ Objective 6.1, "Outline the purpose of appropriate safety and environmental procedures and given a scenario apply them"

30. Which statement is false?

    A. EMI in the radio frequency range is called radio frequency interference (RFI).

    B. Static shielding bags help protect computer components from ESD.

    C. Antistatic gloves prevent static discharge between you and the equipment you are handling.

    D. Antistatic gloves are usually a poor substitute for antistatic bracelets.

    220-701 A+ Objective 6.1, "Outline the purpose of appropriate safety and environmental procedures and given a scenario apply them"

31. Data in data cables that cross an electromagnetic field or that run parallel with power cables can become corrupted by EMI/RFI. What does this cause?

    A. Soft power

    B. Swells

    C. Sags

    D. Crosstalk

    220-701 A+ Objective 6.1, "Outline the purpose of appropriate safety and environmental procedures and given a scenario apply them"

6

32. Crosstalk can be partially controlled by using data cables covered with a protective material. What are these cables called?

    A. Shielded

    B. Twisted pair

    C. Copper

    D. Fiber optic

    220-701 A+ Objective 6.1, "Outline the purpose of appropriate safety and environmental procedures and given a scenario apply them"

33. Which of the following protects equipment against sudden changes in power level, such as spikes from lightning strikes?

    A. Bus riser

    B. Diode

    C. Inverter

    D. Surge protector

    220-701 A+ Objective 6.1, "Outline the purpose of appropriate safety and environmental procedures and given a scenario apply them"

34. Which of the following is the work or energy required to produce one watt of power in one second?

    A. One ampere

    B. One ohm

    C. One joule

    D. One diode

    220-701 A+ Objective 6.1, "Outline the purpose of appropriate safety and environmental procedures and given a scenario apply them"

35. Which of the following is rated as to the amount of joules it can expend before it no longer can work to protect the circuit from the power surge?

    A. Capacitor

    B. Suppressor

    C. Diode

    D. Inverter

    220-701 A+ Objective 6.1, "Outline the purpose of appropriate safety and environmental procedures and given a scenario apply them"

36. Which of the following is the voltage point at which a suppressor begins to absorb or block voltage?

A. Breaking point

B. Clamping voltage

C. Brownout

D. Spike

220-701 A+ Objective 6.1, "Outline the purpose of appropriate safety and environmental procedures and given a scenario apply them"

37. In addition to providing protection against spikes, which of the following regulates, or conditions, power, providing continuous voltage during brownouts?

A. Faraday cage

B. Transformers

C. Multimeters

D. Line conditioners

220-701 A+ Objective 6.1, "Outline the purpose of appropriate safety and environmental procedures and given a scenario apply them"

38. Which of the following provides backup power in the event that the AC fails completely?

A. Uninterruptible power supply

B. Line conditioner

C. Inverter

D. Ground bracelet

220-701 A+ Objective 6.1, "Outline the purpose of appropriate safety and environmental procedures and given a scenario apply them"

39. Which of the following ratings is the theoretical rating that is calculated by multiplying volts by amps and then added up for all the equipment?

A. Volts

B. Amps

C. VA

D. Watt

220-701 A+ Objective 6.1, "Outline the purpose of appropriate safety and environmental procedures and given a scenario apply them"

40. Which statement is false?

    A. When two objects with dissimilar electrical charges touch, electricity passes between them until the dissimilar charges become equal.

    B. You can touch a chip on an expansion card or motherboard, damage the chip with ESD, and never feel, hear, or see the discharge.

    C. To protect the computer against ESD, always ground yourself before touching electronic components, including the hard drive, motherboard, expansion cards, processors, and memory modules.

    D. Always store expansion cards on top of or next to a CRT monitor.

    220-701 A+ Objective 6.1, "Outline the purpose of appropriate safety and environmental procedures and given a scenario apply them"

41. Which of the following, together with a ground mat, provides the best way to guard against ESD?

    A. Diagnostic card

    B. Daughter card

    C. Ground bracelet

    D. Inverter

    220-701 A+ Objective 6.1, "Outline the purpose of appropriate safety and environmental procedures and given a scenario apply them"

42. Which statement is false?

    A. With ATX and BTX cases, residual power is still on even when the power switch on the rear of the case is turned off.

    B. When working on ATX and BTX systems, unplug the power cord and then press the power button to completely drain the power supply.

    C. There is more danger of ESD when the atmosphere is hot and humid.

    D. A ground bracelet is essential equipment when working on a computer.

    220-701 A+ Objective 6.1, "Outline the purpose of appropriate safety and environmental procedures and given a scenario apply them"

43. Which of the following does *not* emit EMI/RFI?

    A. LCD monitors

    B. Cell phones

    C. Microwave ovens

    D. Magnets

    220-701 A+ Objective 6.1, "Outline the purpose of appropriate safety and environmental procedures and given a scenario apply them"

44. If mysterious, intermittent errors persist on a PC, what might you suspect?

    A. Electrostatic discharge

    B. ATX

    C. Spikes

    D. EMI/RFI

    220-701 A+ Objective 6.1, "Outline the purpose of appropriate safety and environmental procedures and given a scenario apply them"

45. Which of the following is the UL standard that applies to surge suppressors? It was first published in 1985 and revised in 1998.

    A. UL 1000

    B. UL 1449

    C. RFI 1000

    D. RFI 1449

    220-701 A+ Objective 6.1, "Outline the purpose of appropriate safety and environmental procedures and given a scenario apply them"

46. Which of the following can come as power strips, wall-mounted units that plug into AC outlets, or consoles designed to sit beneath the monitor on a desktop?

    A. Surge suppressors

    B. Transformers

    C. P1 connectors

    D. Transformers

    220-701 A+ Objective 6.1, "Outline the purpose of appropriate safety and environmental procedures and given a scenario apply them"

47. When passing a circuit board, memory module, or other sensitive component to another person, what should you do?

    A. Stand on a piece of carpet before you pass the component.

    B. Remove all wet clothing before you pass the component.

    C. Ground yourself and then touch the other person before you pass the component.

    D. Touch the other person before you pass the component.

    220-701 A+ Objective 6.1, "Outline the purpose of appropriate safety and environmental procedures and given a scenario apply them"

48. What should always be installed in empty drive bays or slot covers over empty expansion slots to help cut down on EMI between PCs?

    A. Joules

    B. Face plates

    C. Daughter cards

    D. Diagnostic cards

    220-701 A+ Objective 6.1, "Outline the purpose of appropriate safety and environmental procedures and given a scenario apply them"

6

49. Which of the following can be used to detect EMI?

    A. AM radio

    B. CRT monitor

    C. LCD monitor

    D. Soft switch

    220-701 A+ Objective 6.1, "Outline the purpose of appropriate safety and environmental procedures and given a scenario apply them"

50. If EMI in the electrical circuits coming to the PC causes a significant problem, which of the following would you use to filter the electrical noise that causes the EMI?

    A. Transformer

    B. Bus riser

    C. Rectifier

    D. Line conditioner

    220-701 A+ Objective 6.1, "Outline the purpose of appropriate safety and environmental procedures and given a scenario apply them"

Part II

CompTIA A+ 220-702 Practical Applications Exam

Domain 1.0 Hardware

Domain 2.0 Operating Systems

Domain 3.0 Networking

Domain 4.0 Security

1.0

HARDWARE

1. You are in the process of selecting components for a computer that you are assembling. The computer's *form factor* is vital in selecting all of the following components *except* what?

A. Motherboard

B. Power supply

C. Processor

D. Case

220-702 A+ Objective 1.1, "Install, configure, and maintain personal computer components"

2. You would like to determine a power supply's wattage rating for *continuous* operation. How would you calculate this from its *peak* rating?

A. Add about 10 to 15 percent.

B. Subtract about 10 to 15 percent.

C. Add about 20 to 25 percent.

D. Subtract about 20 to 25 percent.

220-702 A+ Objective 1.1, "Install, configure, and maintain personal computer components"

3. A client is asking you about the power consumption of various components in a computer system. Which component typically draws the most power in a system?

A. Video card

B. DVD burner

C. Hard drive

D. Case fan

220-702 A+ Objective 1.1, "Install, configure, and maintain personal computer components"

4. Consider the following system: a desktop system used as a file server, with a high-end motherboard, an Intel processor, a PCI RAID card, four SATA hard drives, a tape drive, a CD drive, a low-end video card, and three fans. What would be the most appropriate power supply rating?

A. 300W

B. 450W

C. 750W

D. 925W

220-702 A+ Objective 1.1, "Install, configure, and maintain personal computer components"

5. Consider the following system: A gaming system with a high-end motherboard and processor, two high-end video cards, two SATA hard drives, a DVD-RW drive and a Blu-ray drive, and four fans. What would be the most appropriate power supply rating?

A. 300W

B. 450W

C. 750W

D. 925W

220-702 A+ Objective 1.1, "Install, configure, and maintain personal computer components"

6. Consider the following system: A basic system with a moderate motherboard and processor, one IDE hard drive, one DVD drive, a moderate video card, and one fan. What would be the most appropriate power supply rating?

A. 300W

B. 450W

C. 750W

D. 925W

220-702 A+ Objective 1.1, "Install, configure, and maintain personal computer components"

7. You have just come in from the cold and need to upgrade the RAM on a customer's computer. To lessen the risk of electrostatic discharge, what should you do?

A. Take off your shoes.

B. Wait a few minutes until you warm up.

C. Dive right in and get started.

D. Touch the heat sink first.

220-702 A+ Objective 1.2, "Detect problems, troubleshoot, and repair/replace computer components"

8. You need to test whether a component such as the video card or SATA drive is getting sufficient power. What is the best tool to use?

A. A duplicate of the same component known to be in working order

B. A power supply tester

C. A multimeter

D. A POST diagnostic card

220-702 A+ Objective 1.4, "Select and use tools"

9. You need to figure out which pins on one end of a cable match the other end. What should you set your multimeter to measure?

A. Voltage

B. Resistance

C. Current

D. Continuity

220-702 A+ Objective 1.4, "Select and use tools"

10. You are rebuilding a computer system. Under what circumstances is it safe to work inside a power supply or monitor?

 A. Provided the system is unplugged and disconnected

 B. Provided you wear an antistatic bracelet or gloves

 C. Provided the system is unplugged and disconnected *and* you wear antistatic protection

 D. None of the above

 220-702 Objective 1.1, "Install, configure, and maintain personal computer components"

11. You are reviewing a list of instructions before your first house call to a client. What is often the first step in working on computer hardware?

 A. Make a diagram of screws and cables as you disassemble it.

 B. Make sure you are grounded with an antistatic bracelet.

 C. Turn off, unplug, and discharge the system.

 D. Back up any important data.

 220-702 Objective 1.1, "Install, configure, and maintain personal computer components"

12. A client has asked you to install a floppy disk drive to read legacy files. A floppy drive cable is characterized by which of the following?

 A. A 34-pin connector and a ribbon connector with a twist

 B. A 40-pin connector ribbon cable

 C. A 40-pin connector with an 80-wire ribbon

 D. A four-pin connector and eight colored wires

 220-702 Objective 1.1, "Install, configure, and maintain personal computer components"

13. You have disassembled and replaced a component in a client's computer. What is the best order for reassembling the computer?

 A. Install cards into the motherboard, install the motherboard, install the drives, install the power supply

 B. Install the drives, install the power supply, install cards into the motherboard, install the motherboard

 C. Install the power supply, install the drives, install the motherboard, install cards into the motherboard

 D. Install the power supply, install cards into the motherboard, install the motherboard, install the drives

 220-702 Objective 1.1, "Install, configure, and maintain personal computer components"

1

14. Your friend Bill describes a computer problem to you. His computer has been working fine since he got it for Christmas about eight months ago, but now the system powers down for no apparent reason while he is working, and usually after he's been working for several hours. He's checked the electrical connection on his power strip, and that isn't the problem. He hasn't noticed any task or application that seems to cause the problem. What's your first diagnosis?

    A. Software-related issue

    B. Overheating from a faulty fan or blockage of air vents

    C. Faulty memory

    D. A problem with the power supply

    220-702 Objective 1.2, "Detect problems, troubleshoot, and repair/replace computer components"

15. Your friend Fred's computer is having problems that you suspect are due to a problem with the power supply. You want to replace it with a new one. Which of the following criteria is *not* a requirement of the new power supply?

    A. Same form factor (ATX, BTX, and so on)

    B. At least as many connectors of each of the necessary types as the old power supply

    C. Identical wattage rating

    D. All of these are essential

    220-702 Objective 1.2, "Detect problems, troubleshoot, and repair/replace computer components"

16. A client is reporting problems with his computer. Which of the following can be caused by a faulty power supply?

    A. Memory errors

    B. Reboots

    C. System hangs

    D. All of the above

    220-702 Objective 1.2, "Detect problems, troubleshoot, and repair/replace computer components"

17. You have recently replaced several components in a system, and now the computer is not booting correctly. To identify what hardware component is causing a startup error, what should you use?

    A. A power supply tester

    B. A POST diagnostic card

    C. A multimeter

    D. Windows diagnostic software

    220-702 Objective 1.4, "Select and use tools"

18. You are attempting to detect interference with your equipment. Which of the following is a good method to detect electromagnetic interference?

    A. Look for strange patterns in a CRT monitor.

    B. Listen to an AM radio tuned to a low frequency.

    C. Listen to an FM radio tuned to a high frequency.

    D. Use a tin-foil hat.

    220-702 Objective 1.4, "Select and use tools"

19. You are configuring a computer for a client who needs a lot of expansion hardware. Which form factor has the largest motherboard size?

    A. ATX

    B. FlexATX

    C. ITX

    D. PicoBTX

    220-702 Objective 1.1, "Install, configure, and maintain personal computer components"

20. The system date and time are incorrect after the PC has been disconnected from power. What might this indicate?

    A. The power supply is about to fail.

    B. The CMOS battery is getting weak.

    C. The system is overclocked.

    D. There is electromagnetic interference.

    220-702 Objective 1.2, "Detect problems, troubleshoot, and repair/replace computer components"

1

21. You have been asked to select components for a new computer. In most cases, what component is your most important choice in configuring a computer?

    A. The motherboard

    B. The hard drive

    C. The power supply

    D. The memory

    220-702 Objective 1.1, "Install, configure, and maintain personal computer components"

22. Which of the following is *not* an occasion where you might want to flash the ROM BIOS?

    A. The processor has been upgraded.

    B. A feature such as a USB port has stopped working.

    C. The motherboard has become unstable.

    D. You want to monitor the CPU temperature.

    220-702 Objective 1.1, "Install, configure, and maintain personal computer components"

23. You are asked to update the BIOS on a motherboard whose manual says it allows for an express BIOS update. How is an express BIOS update done?

    A. By booting the computer while connected to the Internet and holding down a key combination

    B. By downloading and running an application from Windows

    C. By booting from a floppy disk

    D. Automatically, without any need for user or technician intervention

    220-702 Objective 1.1, "Install, configure, and maintain personal computer components"

24. Your client set a power-on password in the BIOS, but she has forgotten it. How can you recover access to the computer?

    A. Through a special application in Windows.

    B. Through a special key combination at boot-up.

    C. By setting a jumper on the motherboard.

    D. You cannot recover access; the motherboard must be replaced.

    220-702 Objective 1.1, "Install, configure, and maintain personal computer components"

25. You are replacing a motherboard. When should the processor cooler be installed?

    A. Before the processor is installed and before the motherboard is installed

    B. Before the processor is installed and after the motherboard is installed

    C. After the processor is installed and according to the motherboard manufacturer's instructions

    D. After the RAM is installed

    220-702 Objective 1.1, "Install, configure, and maintain personal computer components"

26. You have installed a new processor cooler on a motherboard. The power cable from the CPU fan should be connected to what?

    A. The P1 main power connection

    B. A Molex-style connection from the power supply

    C. A SATA-style connection from the power supply

    D. The appropriately labeled pins on the motherboard

    220-702 Objective 1.1, "Install, configure, and maintain personal computer components"

27. You have installed a floppy drive in a client's computer and need to update the BIOS. How is the BIOS setup program accessed?

    A. By pressing a key or combination of keys during boot-up

    B. By setting jumpers on the motherboard

    C. By running an application from Windows OS

    D. By booting off a floppy or CD

    220-702 Objective 1.1, "Install, configure, and maintain personal computer components"

28. You need to change the order in which the system tries to start up from certain devices. In what section of the BIOS settings is this likely to be configured?

    A. Main

    B. Power

    C. Boot

    D. Advanced

    220-702 Objective 1.1, "Install, configure, and maintain personal computer components"

29. One of the slots on the motherboard for a computer you are assembling is labeled "AGP." What goes in this slot?

    A. An auxiliary power distribution board

    B. A video card

    C. Memory

    D. The central processing unit

    220-702 Objective 1.1, "Install, configure, and maintain personal computer components"

30. When troubleshooting a motherboard, you discover the network port no longer works. What is the best and least expensive solution to this problem?

    A. Replace the motherboard.

    B. Disable the network port and install a network card in an expansion slot.

    C. Use a wireless network device in a USB port to connect to a wireless network.

    D. Return the motherboard to the factory for repair.

    220-702 Objective 1.2, "Detect problems, troubleshoot, and repair/replace computer components"

31. You have been asked to select a processor to match a given motherboard. Which of the following is the *least* likely to constrain your choice?

    A. Form factor

    B. Socket type

    C. Front side bus speed

    D. Memory type compatibility

    220-702 Objective 1.1, "Install, configure, and maintain personal computer components"

32. You are installing a processor and cooler onto a motherboard. You purchased the processor and cooler separately, and the cooler does not have thermal compound preapplied. How much thermal compound should you use?

    A. Just a small dot; a few drops

    B. Just enough to create a thin layer over the whole surface of the processor

    C. Enough to create a thick layer over the whole surface of the processor

    D. The whole package

    220-702 Objective 1.2, "Detect problems, troubleshoot, and repair/replace computer components"

1

33. You have just installed a new processor and cooler in a system. When you power up the system, the power comes on and you hear fans and see lights, but the system fails to work. What is the most likely problem?

    A. The power supply is not installed correctly.

    B. The CPU cooler is not installed correctly.

    C. The processor is not seated correctly.

    D. The RAM is not seated correctly.

    220-702 Objective 1.2, "Detect problems, troubleshoot, and repair/replace computer components"

34. You have just installed a new processor and cooler in a system. When you power up the system, the system comes up and begins the boot process but suddenly turns off before the boot is complete. What is the most likely problem?

    A. The power supply is not installed correctly.

    B. The CPU cooler is not installed correctly.

    C. The processor is not seated correctly.

    D. The RAM is not seated correctly.

    220-702 Objective 1.2, "Detect problems, troubleshoot, and repair/replace computer components"

35. You are installing a new processor in a motherboard. What is the proper way to hold the processor while placing it in the socket?

    A. Carefully by the edges

    B. With needlenosed pliers

    C. Firmly gripping on the top and bottom

    D. Any of the above

    220-702 Objective 1.1, "Install, configure, and maintain personal computer components"

36. You are installing a processor and cooler for a client. It does not already have thermal compound applied. Where should the thermal compound be applied?

    A. To the top surface of the processor

    B. To the bottom surface of the CPU cooler

    C. One of the above, but not both

    D. Both of the above

    220-702 Objective 1.1, "Install, configure, and maintain personal computer components"

37. A client is trying to decide between asking you to build an Intel-based system and an AMD-based system. What are the major differences in procedure for installing AMD versus Intel processors?

A. AMD processors have pins, whereas Intel processors have contact pads.

B. Intel sockets use a ZIF lever, whereas AMD sockets do not.

C. Intel-based systems need larger heat sinks.

D. There are no major differences in installation procedure between Intel and AMD processors.

220-702 Objective 1.1, "Install, configure, and maintain personal computer components"

38. Your client places a priority on energy conservation and asks you to configure her BIOS to reduce consumption. What ACPI mode offers the most energy savings?

A. S1

B. S2

C. S3

D. S4

220-702 Objective 1.1, "Install, configure, and maintain personal computer components"

39. Your client places a priority on energy conservation and asks you to configure her BIOS to reduce consumption. What CPU P state offers the most energy savings?

A. P0

B. P1

C. P2

D. P3

220-702 Objective 1.1, "Install, configure, and maintain personal computer components"

40. Your client places a priority on energy conservation and asks you to configure her BIOS to reduce consumption. What setting saves power by lowering the CPU frequency and voltage?

A. P states

B. Enhanced Intel SpeedStep Technology

C. AMD PowerNow!

D. All of the above

220-702 Objective 1.1, "Install, configure, and maintain personal computer components"

41. Your client places a priority on energy conservation and asks you to configure her BIOS to reduce consumption. What ACPI mode suspends the computer to RAM?

A. S1

B. S2

C. S3

D. S4

220-702 Objective 1.1, "Install, configure, and maintain personal computer components"

1

42. Your client places a priority on energy conservation but also wants his computer to be responsive. From which ACPI CPU C state does it take the longest for the processor to wake up?

    A. C0

    B. C2

    C. C4

    D. C6

    220-702 Objective 1.1, "Install, configure, and maintain personal computer components"

43. You have built your first computer. You have installed all the components and checked the connections. You plug in the power cord and turn on the power switch on the power supply at the back of the computer, and you immediately hear a faint whine. You turn the switch back off, unplug the power supply, and carefully check all the power connections. Everything looks okay. You plug the power supply back in and switch it on again, only to hear the same whine. What is the most likely cause of the problem?

    A. No problem—that's normal. Full speed ahead!

    B. A short in the system—too much power is being drawn.

    C. Not enough power to the power supply—perhaps a problem with the power strip or building wiring.

    D. A faulty case fan.

    220-702 Objective 1.2, "Detect problems, troubleshoot, and repair/replace computer components"

44. Your friend is concerned that her computer system may be overheating. Which of the following is *not* a symptom that the system is overheating?

    A. The system hangs or freezes at odd times.

    B. The system freezes just a few moments after the boot starts.

    C. Nothing happens when you push the power button.

    D. You cannot feel air being pulled into the case.

    220-702 Objective 1.2, "Detect problems, troubleshoot, and repair/replace computer components"

45. You are investigating a computer that you suspect is overheating. Just after a system freeze, you go into the BIOS and check the reported temperature. What temperature should not be exceeded for normal operation?

    A. 100° F

    B. 212° F

    C. 98.6° F

    D. 38° F

    220-702 Objective 1.2, "Detect problems, troubleshoot, and repair/replace computer components"

46. You are checking the fans on a system you suspect is overheating. In which direction should a fan at the rear of the case blow?

    A. Toward the processor

    B. Out of the case

    C. Into the case

    D. Toward the power supply unit

    220-702 Objective 1.2, "Detect problems, troubleshoot, and repair/replace computer components"

47. You are checking the fans on a system you suspect is overheating. In which direction should a fan at the front of the case blow?

    A. Toward the processor

    B. Out of the case

    C. Into the case

    D. Toward the power supply unit

    220-702 Objective 1.2, "Detect problems, troubleshoot, and repair/replace computer components"

48. You are installing memory in a motherboard with four DIMM slots, colored (in order) blue, blue, blue, black. You install an identical 1-GB DIMM in each slot (with type, speed, voltage, and other specifications that match the motherboard). In which mode will the memory be accessed?

    A. Single channel

    B. Dual channel

    C. Triple channel

    D. Quadruple channel

    220-702 Objective 1.1, "Install, configure, and maintain personal computer components"

49. You are installing memory in a motherboard with four DIMM slots, colored (in order) blue, blue, blue, black. You install an identical 1-GB DIMM in each slot *except* the last one, with type, speed, voltage, and other specifications that match the motherboard. In which mode will the memory be accessed?

    A. Single channel

    B. Dual channel

    C. Triple channel

    D. Quadruple channel

    220-702 Objective 1.1, "Install, configure, and maintain personal computer components"

1

50. You are installing additional memory in a motherboard. It currently has two 512-MB modules of PC2-4200 (533-MHz) unbuffered memory, but the motherboard documentation states that it also accepts PC2-5400 (667-MHz) memory and a maximum of 4 GB. You happen to have two 1-GB DIMMs of PC2-5400 unbuffered memory on hand. Assuming the other specifications match, will they work in this system?

    A. Yes, but only if the currently installed PC-4200 memory is removed.

    B. Yes, but it will run at only 533 MHz.

    C. Yes, and it will run at 667 MHz.

    D. Not at all.

    220-702 Objective 1.1, "Install, configure, and maintain personal computer components"

51. You are installing additional memory in a motherboard. It currently has two 512-MB modules of PC2-4200 (533-MHz) unbuffered memory, but the motherboard documentation says it also accepts PC2-5400 (667-MHz) memory and a maximum of 4 GB. You happen to have two 1-GB DIMMs of PC2-5400 memory lying around, but it is labeled buffered. Assuming the other specifications match, will they work in this system?

    A. Yes, but only if the currently installed PC-4200 memory is removed.

    B. Yes, but it will run at only 533 MHz.

    C. Yes, and it will run at 667 MHz.

    D. Not at all.

    220-702 Objective 1.1, "Install, configure, and maintain personal computer components"

52. You are installing a DDR2 DIMM onto a motherboard. How should the DIMM be installed?

    A. By hand, straight down until clips pop into place.

    B. By hand, sliding into the slot at an angle and rotating up.

    C. With a flat-head screwdriver, being careful not to overtorque.

    D. It varies by motherboard manufacturer—check the documentation for the motherboard in question.

    220-702 Objective 1.1, "Install, configure, and maintain personal computer components"

53. Your friend has a motherboard that supports up to 8 GB of dual-channel DDR2 memory in his Windows XP gaming computer. He currently has four 1-GB DIMMs installed, but he wants to replace them with 2-GB DIMMs for better gaming performance. What would you suggest?

    A. Don't bother.

    B. Make sure to get high-quality buffered memory.

    C. Maybe start by replacing just two of the DIMMs to see if that gives enough of a boost in performance.

    D. Go for it!

    220-702 Objective 1.1, "Install, configure, and maintain personal computer components"

54. You are adding memory to a laptop. You probably want to shop for which of these?

    A. DIMM

    B. SO-DIMM

    C. RIMM

    D. SIMM

    220-702 Objective 1.3, "Install, configure, detect problems, troubleshoot, and repair/replace laptop components"

55. You are assembling a computer from spare parts. The motherboard you have supports dual channel PC2-6400 unbuffered memory in sizes up to 2 GB per DIMM, and you've been able to scrounge up four PC2-6400 DIMMs. Most of the specifications are the same, but they're different sizes: one 256 MB, one 512 MB, one 1 GB, and one 2 GB. If you install all four in the motherboard, will they work?

    A. No way.

    B. Probably, but you'll only get 256 MB out of each one, for a total of 1 GB of RAM.

    C. Probably, but you'll only get single channeling.

    D. It would be nice if they were identical, but you will probably still get dual channel performance of all 3.75 GB.

    220-702 Objective 1.1, "Install, configure, and maintain personal computer components"

56. You are installing a CPU fan on a motherboard, but the CPU fan connector has only three pins, and the motherboard's header has four. Can it still be connected?

    A. Yes; it will make no difference.

    B. Yes, but it will run more slowly.

    C. Yes, but it will always run at full speed.

    D. No.

    220-702 Objective 1.1, "Install, configure, and maintain personal computer components"

57. You upgrade a system's PCIe video card to a recently released high-performance card. Now users complain to you that Windows Vista hangs a lot and gives errors. What is the most likely source of the problem?

    A. Overheating.

    B. Windows does not support the new card.

    C. The drivers for the card need updating.

    D. Memory is faulty.

    220-702 Objective 1.2, "Detect problems, troubleshoot, and repair/replace computer components"

1

58. You are examining a motherboard for which you want to purchase memory. The board has four slots for DIMMs: two colored yellow and two colored black. What does this suggest?

A. The board accepts two different kinds of memory.

B. The board accepts dual-channel memory.

C. The board accepts a maximum of 4 GB of memory.

D. The board has two processors.

220-702 Objective 1.1, "Install, configure, and maintain personal computer components

59. You are examining a motherboard for which you want to purchase memory. The board has four slots for DIMMs: three colored blue and one colored black. What does this suggest?

A. The board accepts two different kinds of memory.

B. The board accepts triple-channel memory.

C. The black slot is for L2 memory, and the blue slots are for L3.

D. You must install one or three DIMMs.

220-702 Objective 1.1, "Install, configure, and maintain personal computer components"

60. You are installing memory in a motherboard with four DIMM slots, colored (in order) blue, blue, blue, black. Assuming the same compatible memory type and speed, which of these configurations would be best?

A. 1 GB, 1 GB, 512 MB, 512 MB

B. 1 GB, 1 GB, 1 GB, empty

C. 512 MB, 1 GB, 512 MB, 1 GB

D. Empty, 1 GB, 1 GB, 1 GB

220-702 Objective 1.1, "Install, configure, and maintain personal computer components"

61. You are installing memory in a motherboard with four DIMM slots, colored (in order) blue, black, blue, black. Assuming the same compatible memory type and speed, which of these configurations would be best?

A. 1 GB, 1 GB, 512 MB, 512 MB

B. 1 GB, 1 GB, 1 GB, empty

C. 512 MB, 1 GB, 512 MB, 1 GB

D. Empty, 1 GB, 1 GB, 1 GB

220-702 Objective 1.1, "Install, configure, and maintain personal computer components"

62. You need to find out how much RAM is installed in a system. What command do you enter in the Vista Start Search box or the XP Run dialog box to launch the System Information utility?

A. Msinfo32

B. SysInfo

C. MemInfo

D. SysInfo64

220-702 Objective 1.1, "Install, configure, and maintain personal computer components"

63. You need to upgrade memory in a system but don't have the motherboard documentation available. You peek in the case and notice that the board has four DIMM slots. Three are yellow and one is black. What type of DIMM does the board likely use?

    A. DDR-SDRAM

    B. DDR2-SDRAM

    C. DDR3-SDRAM

    D. Rambus

    220-702 Objective 1.1, "Install, configure, and maintain personal computer components"

64. Your friend asks you to help him pick out a hard drive for a new desktop system he is assembling to use for e-mail, the Web, office work, and light gaming applications. What is the reasonable "default" hard drive interface to choose for this system, barring any exceptional needs?

    A. PATA

    B. SATA

    C. SCSI

    D. SSD

    220-702 Objective 1.1, "Install, configure, and maintain personal computer components"

65. You have been asked to install a SATA hard drive containing important data into a system with an older motherboard that does not have SATA connections. Is this possible? If so, what is the best way to do it?

    A. No, this is not possible.

    B. Use a PATA-to-SATA converter.

    C. Install an expansion card that provides SATA ports.

    D. Connect it using an external USB connection.

    220-702 Objective 1.1, "Install, configure, and maintain personal computer components"

66. You are installing a SATA hard drive, and you notice that it has a bank of jumpers on the back. How should you set the jumpers?

    A. You probably should leave them alone, as they were configured at the factory.

    B. You should check the instructions to set the jumper for "master."

    C. You should set the jumper to indicate whether this is a RAID drive.

    D. You should set the jumper according to what revision of SATA is being used.

    220-702 Objective 1.1, "Install, configure, and maintain personal computer components"

67. You have installed a new hard drive and are now configuring it in Windows. For most situations, what is the most appropriate choice for the file system?

    A. FAT32

    B. NTFS

    C. ext3

    D. ATAPI

    220-702 Objective 1.1, "Install, configure, and maintain personal computer components"

1

68. You are installing a parallel ATA drive with a color-coded parallel ATA 80-conductor cable. The blue end should be connected to what?

    A. The motherboard

    B. The first drive

    C. The second drive

    D. Whichever device is closer to the motherboard

    220-702 Objective 1.1, "Install, configure, and maintain personal computer components"

69. You are installing a PATA hard drive in a system where it will be the only drive connected to the cable. What color connector plugs into the drive?

    A. Blue

    B. Black

    C. Grey

    D. None of the above

    220-702 Objective 1.1, "Install, configure, and maintain personal computer components"

70. You are installing a PATA hard drive on the same channel as an ATAPI CD drive. Which device should be the master?

    A. The hard drive.

    B. The CD drive.

    C. The motherboard.

    D. It doesn't matter.

    220-702 Objective 1.1, "Install, configure, and maintain personal computer components"

71. You are configuring a system with a tape drive, a CD drive, and two hard drives, all IDE. How should they be arranged?

    A. Primary channel: hard drive, CD drive; secondary channel: hard drive, tape drive

    B. Primary channel: hard drive, hard drive; secondary channel: CD drive, tape drive

    C. Primary channel: CD drive, tape drive; secondary channel: hard drive, hard drive

    D. Primary channel: tape drive, hard drive; secondary channel: CD drive, hard drive

    220-702 Objective 1.1, "Install, configure, and maintain personal computer components"

72. You are configuring a system with a PATA hard drive, an IDE DVD drive, and an IDE CD drive. What device should get a channel to itself, and which channel should be used?

    A. DVD drive, primary channel

    B. Hard drive, primary channel

    C. Hard drive, secondary channel

    D. CD drive, secondary channel

    220-702 Objective 1.1, "Install, configure, and maintain personal computer components"

73. You are configuring a system with a fast PATA hard drive for the operating system, a large PATA hard drive for data, and an IDE CD drive. What device should get a channel to itself, and which channel?

    A. OS hard drive, primary channel

    B. CD drive, secondary channel

    C. Data hard drive, primary channel

    D. Data hard drive, secondary channel

    220-702 Objective 1.1, "Install, configure, and maintain personal computer components"

74. You notice the jumpers on an IDE hard drive in a computer you are servicing has the jumpers set to "CSEL." To use the hard drive in this configuration, what else must you do?

    A. Set the other drive on the channel to "master."

    B. Set the other drive on the channel to "slave."

    C. Make sure it is the only device on the channel.

    D. Use a cable-select data cable.

    220-702 Objective 1.1, "Install, configure, and maintain personal computer components"

75. You are asked to install a new hard drive in a case that already has several drives in it. A standard desktop hard drive is the same width as what device(s)?

    A. A DVD drive

    B. A floppy disk drive

    C. Both of the above

    D. Neither of the above

    220-702 Objective 1.1, "Install, configure, and maintain personal computer components"

76. You need to install a hard drive into a computer that does not have any more 3.5-inch bays open. To install a hard drive in a wide bay, what do you need?

    A. An extension cable for the power connection

    B. A cable-select data cable

    C. A universal bay kit

    D. A SATA-to-PATA adapter

    220-702 Objective 1.1, "Install, configure, and maintain personal computer components"

77. You have been asked to configure a RAID array. RAID can be implemented in which of the following?

    A. On many motherboards

    B. On a RAID controller expansion card

    C. In Windows

    D. All of the above

    220-702 Objective 1.1, "Install, configure, and maintain personal computer components"

1

78. You are configuring a motherboard for RAID 5. How is RAID enabled?

    A. The motherboard automatically detects that drives have been connected to RAID interfaces.

    B. By setting jumpers or DIP switches on the motherboard.

    C. By setting jumpers on the hard drives to be used in the array.

    D. In BIOS setup.

    220-702 Objective 1.1, "Install, configure, and maintain personal computer components"

79. You are installing an internal floppy drive in a system. The side of the connector with the colored edge on the end of the cable with the twist goes where?

    A. Motherboard, pin 1

    B. Motherboard, pin 34

    C. Drive, pin 1

    D. Drive, pin 34

    220-702 Objective 1.1, "Install, configure, and maintain personal computer components"

80. Often when a hard drive is not functioning properly, the user's first priority is the data. In these cases, what is a good first step in troubleshooting the drive?

    A. If another drive in the system is working, swap the trouble hard drive with the working one to diagnose if the hard drive works connected to a different connector.

    B. Send the drive to a data recovery specialist.

    C. Remove the problem drive and install it as a second drive in a working system.

    D. Check the BIOS setting to make sure autodetection is enabled.

    220-702 Objective 1.2, "Detect problems, troubleshoot, and repair/replace computer components"

81. You are diagnosing a hard drive problem and conclude that the drive is not being found by BIOS at POST. Which of these is *not* a possible cause of the error?

    A. A loose connection at one end of the data cable.

    B. Incorrect jumper settings on the drive.

    C. BIOS autodetection is not enabled.

    D. The bootloader has been corrupted.

    220-702 Objective 1.2, "Detect problems, troubleshoot, and repair/replace computer components"

82. You are diagnosing a computer that won't boot off the hard drive. You would like to determine whether the problem is with the hard drive subsystem or with the motherboard. What is a good, convenient test to determine this?

    A. Replace the motherboard.

    B. Check the power and data cable connections on the hard drive and try again.

    C. Try to boot from another medium, such as a bootable recovery CD.

    D. Inspect the drive for physical damage.

    220-702 Objective 1.2, "Detect problems, troubleshoot, and repair/replace computer components"

83. You are working on an older computer whose hard drive whines loudly when you first turn on the computer. What should you do?

   A. Turn the computer off and let it sit, preferably over night.

   B. Leave the computer running and make arrangements to get any important data copied to another drive.

   C. Turn the computer off and check all power connections.

   D. Immediately disconnect the drive, and then shut down the computer.

   220-702 Objective 1.2, "Detect problems, troubleshoot, and repair/replace computer components"

84. You are working with a system with a floppy disk, and it gives this error when you boot: "Non-system disk or disk error. Replace and strike any key when ready. No operating system found." What does this mean, and what should you do?

   A. You are trying to boot from a disk that is not bootable. Try a different disk or remove the disk and boot from the hard drive.

   B. The disk is not formatted. Try formatting the disk or try a different disk.

   C. The disk is write-protected. Close the write-protection switch on the disk.

   D. The sector markings on the disk are fading or corrupted. Ignore the error, but don't trust the disk with important data.

   220-702 Objective 1.2, "Detect problems, troubleshoot, and repair/replace computer components"

85. A client wants you to replace a failed hard drive without powering down the system. This is only possible if what is true?

   A. The drive supports S.M.A.R.T.

   B. The drive has DMA enabled.

   C. The drive is hot-swappable or hot-pluggable.

   D. It is an IDE drive.

   220-702 Objective 1.2, "Detect problems, troubleshoot, and repair/replace computer components"

86. A client can afford two hard disks, and his highest priority is to have a lot of capacity and high performance. What RAID level would be most appropriate?

   A. RAID 0

   B. RAID 1

   C. RAID 0+1

   D. RAID 5

   220-702 Objective 1.1, "Install, configure, and maintain personal computer components"

87. A client can afford two hard disks, but she is more concerned with data security than capacity or performance—she can't afford to lose her data, even if a hard drive fails. What RAID level would be most appropriate?

    A. RAID 0

    B. RAID 1

    C. RAID 0+1

    D. RAID 5

    220-702 Objective 1.1, "Install, configure, and maintain personal computer components"

88. A client can afford three or four hard drives but wants to get as much capacity as possible while still maintaining fault tolerance if a disk goes bad. What RAID level would be most appropriate?

    A. RAID 0

    B. RAID 1

    C. RAID 0+1

    D. RAID 5

    220-702 Objective 1.1, "Install, configure, and maintain personal computer components"

89. You are installing a single IDE drive in a computer. You open it and notice that the motherboard has one blue IDE connector and one black IDE connector (both presently unoccupied). Which one should you use?

    A. Blue.

    B. Black.

    C. Either one is fine.

    D. Use the one that matches the color of the hard drive's interface.

    220-702 Objective 1.1, "Install, configure, and maintain personal computer components"

90. You install a hard drive and then turn on the PC for the first time. You access BIOS setup and see that the drive is not recognized. Which of the following do you do next?

    A. Turn off the PC, open the case, and verify that the memory modules on the motherboard have not become loose.

    B. Turn off the PC, open the case, and verify that the data cable and power cable are connected correctly and jumpers on the drive are set correctly.

    C. Verify that BIOS autodetection is enabled.

    D. Reboot the PC and enter BIOS setup again to see if it now recognizes the drive.

    220-702 Objective 1.1, "Install, configure, and maintain personal computer components"

91. You want to set up your desktop system to use a solid state drive, but the only solid state drives you can find are 2.5-inch drives intended for laptops. What should you do?

    A. Buy a laptop computer with a solid state drive.

    B. Buy a bay adapter that will allow you to install a 2.5-inch drive in a desktop case bay.

    C. Flash BIOS so that your system will support a laptop hard drive.

    D. Use a special SATA controller card that will support a laptop hard drive.

    220-702 Objective 1.1, "Install, configure, and maintain personal computer components"

92. You want to enable or disable a Firewire or USB port or configure a USB port to use high-speed USB, original USB, or both. Where is this done?

    A. With jumpers or DIP switches on the motherboard

    B. In BIOS setup

    C. With Windows Device Manager

    D. None of the above

    220-702 Objective 1.1, "Install, configure, and maintain personal computer components"

93. You are configuring a new USB peripheral for use in Windows. What should be your first step?

    A. Read the documentation to decide if you install the drivers first or plug in the device first.

    B. Install the application software to use the device.

    C. Verify that Device Manager recognizes that a USB or IEEE 1394 controller is present and reports no errors with the port.

    D. Power down and unplug the computer.

    220-702 Objective 1.1, "Install, configure, and maintain personal computer components"

94. You are preparing to install a PCIe-1x SATA adapter card into a motherboard. You notice that the only unoccupied PCIe slots are longer than the card you need to install. What should you do?

    A. Connect the card to an unused SATA connector.

    B. Insert the card into one of the longer PCIe slots—it will still work.

    C. Remove one of the existing expansion cards to make room for the new one.

    D. Replace the motherboard with one with more expansion slots.

    220-702 Objective 1.1, "Install, configure, and maintain personal computer components"

95. You are installing a PCI expansion card. How should a PCI expansion card be seated?

    A. Straight down into the slot until it snaps in

    B. Gently rocked from side to side until it slides down

    C. From front to back

    D. From back to front

    220-702 Objective 1.1, "Install, configure, and maintain personal computer components"

1

96. You have installed a new video card into a system that previously used an embedded video adapter. When you first power up the system, you hear a whining sound. What is most likely the problem?

    A. The card is not getting enough power. Make sure the card's supplemental 6- or 8-pin power connector is connected. The power supply might be inadequate.

    B. There is a conflict with the onboard video—make sure onboard video is disabled.

    C. BIOS cannot detect a video card—make sure the card is securely seated.

    D. Try updating drivers for the video card, the motherboard, or the sound card, and install the latest version of DirectX.

    220-702 Objective 1.1, "Install, configure, and maintain personal computer components"

97. You have installed a new video card into a system that previously used an embedded video adapter. When you first start up the system, you see nothing but a black screen. What is the most likely problem?

    A. The card is not getting enough power. Make sure the card's supplemental 6- or 8-pin power connector is connected. The power supply might be inadequate.

    B. There is a conflict with the onboard video—make sure onboard video is disabled.

    C. BIOS cannot detect a video card—make sure the card is securely seated.

    D. Try updating drivers for the video card, the motherboard, or the sound card, and install the latest version of DirectX.

    220-702 Objective 1.1, "Install, configure, and maintain personal computer components"

98. You have installed a new video card into a system that previously used an embedded video adapter. When you first power up the system, you hear a series of beeps. What is the most likely problem?

    A. The card is not getting enough power. Make sure the card's supplemental 6- or 8-pin power connector is connected. The power supply might be inadequate.

    B. There is a conflict with the onboard video—make sure onboard video is disabled.

    C. BIOS cannot detect a video card—make sure the card is securely seated. The video slot or video card might be bad.

    D. Try updating drivers for the video card, the motherboard, or the sound card, and install the latest version of DirectX.

    220-702 Objective 1.1, "Install, configure, and maintain personal computer components"

99. You have installed a new video card into a system that previously used an embedded video adapter. You are finding that some games crash or lock up when you run them. What is most likely the problem?

    A. The card is not getting enough power. Make sure the card's supplemental 6- or 8-pin power connector is connected. The power supply might be inadequate.

    B. There is a conflict with the onboard video—make sure onboard video is disabled.

    C. BIOS cannot detect a video card—make sure the card is securely seated.

    D. Try updating drivers for the video card, the motherboard, or the sound card, and install the latest version of DirectX.

    220-702 Objective 1.1, "Install, configure, and maintain personal computer components"

100. You have solved a problem with a device by swapping the data cable to the device with a different one; now the device works. What should be your next step?

    A. Close the case.

    B. Make sure the cable is tucked away so it doesn't interfere with airflow in the case.

    C. Mark the cable as bad so no one else tries to use it.

    D. Try the first cable again to make sure the problem was not just a loose connection.

    220-702 Objective 1.2, "Detect problems, troubleshoot, and repair/replace computer components"

101. You plug a new scanner into a USB port on your Windows XP system. When you first turn on the scanner, what should you expect to see?

    A. A message displayed by the scanner software telling you to reboot your system

    B. The Found New Hardware Wizard launching

    C. Your system automatically rebooting

    D. An error message from the USB controller

    220-702 Objective 1.1, "Install, configure, and maintain personal computer components"

102. You are connecting a 2.1 stereo/subwoofer speaker system with a single mine-jack cable to a computer with six sound ports. Into which color sound port should you plug the speakers?

    A. Light blue

    B. Lime green

    C. Pink

    D. Yellow-orange

    220-702 Objective 1.1, "Install, configure, and maintain personal computer components"

103. You are installing an internal media card reader. What internal interface will such a device probably use to connect to the motherboard?

    A. IDE

    B. SATA

    C. USB

    D. SDHC

    220-702 Objective 1.1, "Install, configure, and maintain personal computer components"

104. You have installed an optical drive into a system running Windows XP. What optical drive requires additional software not included with Windows XP to operate?

　　A. CD-ROM drive

　　B. CD-RW burner

　　C. DVD-ROM drive

　　D. DVD-R burner

　　220-702 Objective 1.1, "Install, configure, and maintain personal computer components"

105. You have just upgraded your computer from Windows XP to Windows Vista. Now your system has no sound. What should you do first?

　　A. Check Device Manager to see if the sound card is recognized and has no errors.

　　B. Reinstall Windows XP.

　　C. Download Windows XP drivers for the sound card from the manufacturer's Web site.

　　D. Use Device Manager to uninstall the sound card.

　　220-702 Objective 1.2, "Detect problems, troubleshoot, and repair/replace computer components"

106. To verify network hardware and solve problems with hardware, what step should you take first?

　　A. Determine whether other computers on the network are having trouble with their connections.

　　B. Check the network cable at both ends to make sure it is not damaged.

　　C. Open the case to make sure the NIC is securely seated in the expansion slot.

　　D. Check the status indicator lights on the NIC or the motherboard Ethernet port.

　　220-702 Objective 1.2, "Detect problems, troubleshoot, and repair/replace computer components"

107. You are shopping online for a replacement hard drive for a notebook computer. What is the standard size for a notebook hard drive?

　　A. 3.5 inches

　　B. 2.5 inches

　　C. 5.25 inches

　　D. 250 Gigabytes

　　220-702 Objective 1.3, "Install, configure, detect problems, troubleshoot, and repair/replace laptop components"

108. You are replacing the hard drive in a notebook computer. How do you remove the old hard drive?

  A. Unscrew two screws on the bottom left of the case (on the left when bottom-up), and then lift the panel to access the hard drive.

  B. Remove the battery, and then unscrew the retaining screw on the side of the battery bay. Slide the hard drive out.

  C. Pull the tabs to lift the keyboard, and then remove the four screws holding the guard over the hard drive.

  D. It depends; each notebook computer is different.

  220-702 Objective 1.3, "Install, configure, detect problems, troubleshoot, and repair/replace laptop components"

109. You are servicing the wireless Ethernet card in a notebook computer. How can you tell the difference between a MiniPCI slot and a MiniPCIe slot?

  A. The MiniPCIe slot is smaller than the MiniPCI slot, and the MiniPCI slot has clips to hold in the card, which the MiniPCIe slot does not have.

  B. The MiniPCI slot is smaller than the MiniPCIe slot, and the MiniPCI slot has clips to hold in the card, which the MiniPCIe slot does not have.

  C. The MiniPCIe slot is smaller than the MiniPCI slot, and the MiniPCIe slot has clips to hold in the card, which the MiniPCI slot does not have.

  D. The MiniPCI slot is smaller than the MiniPCIe slot, and the MiniPCIe slot has clips to hold in the card, which the MiniPCI slot does not have.

  220-702 Objective 1.3, "Install, configure, detect problems, troubleshoot, and repair/replace laptop components"

110. You are choosing expansion components for a notebook computer. What is the difference between Bluetooth 1.0 and Bluetooth 2.0?

  A. Bluetooth 2.0 is faster than Bluetooth 1.0, but it uses more power.

  B. Bluetooth 2.0 is faster than Bluetooth 1.0 and uses less power.

  C. Bluetooth 2.0 is the same speed as Bluetooth 1.0, but it uses less power.

  D. Bluetooth 2.0 cards take up less space than Bluetooth 1.0 cards.

  220-702 Objective 1.3, "Install, configure, detect problems, troubleshoot, and repair/replace laptop components"

1

111. You are diagnosing a problem with the display on a notebook computer. The display is dim, even if you adjust the brightness, but you can make out the expected image if you look closely. If you connect the notebook computer to an external monitor, it works fine with the external monitor. What should you suspect to be the problem?

A. The LCD panel

B. The video inverter

C. The video card

D. The display bezel

220-702 Objective 1.3, "Install, configure, detect problems, troubleshoot, and repair/replace laptop components"

112. You are servicing an internal component in a client's notebook computer. You have removed the AC adapter, any removable media, any expansion cards, and any peripherals. What other component(s) should you remove before servicing any internals?

A. Any extra memory modules

B. The keyboard

C. The display

D. The battery

220-702 Objective 1.3, "Install, configure, detect problems, troubleshoot, and repair/replace laptop components"

113. You have been asked to help a client perform routine maintenance on her inkjet printer. How can you clean the nozzles and align the cartridges?

A. From the Services tab on the printer's Properties window.

B. From the utility program that came with the printer's software.

C. Using the maintenance menu on the printer.

D. Any of the above may be applicable depending on the printer.

220-702 Objective 1.5, "Detect and resolve common printer issues"

114. A laser printer you are responsible for maintaining has just begun to display a low toner warning. What can you do to redistribute the toner while you wait for a replacement cartridge to arrive?

A. Select the appropriate option from the maintenance menu in the printer's built-in software.

B. Remove the toner cartridge and rapidly shake it.

C. Remove the toner cartridge and gently rock it back and forth.

D. Brush the surface of the toner cartridge with a cotton swab or paper towel.

220-702 Objective 1.5, "Detect and resolve common printer issues"

2.0

OPERATING SYSTEMS

1. When booting a computer, you hear two beeps followed by three, four, or five beeps during POST. What has most likely happened?

   A. The processor has overheated.

   B. There is a RAM error.

   C. The embedded keyboard or video controller failed.

   D. There is a serious problem with the motherboard's system bus, timer, BIOS setup chip, or DMA.

   220-702 A+ Objective 2.4, "Evaluate and resolve common issues"

2. When booting a computer, you hear three beeps followed by two, three, or four beeps during POST. What has most likely happened?

   A. The processor has overheated.

   B. There is a RAM error.

   C. The embedded keyboard or video controller failed.

   D. There is a serious problem with the motherboard's system bus, timer, BIOS setup chip, or DMA.

   220-702 A+ Objective 2.4, "Evaluate and resolve common issues"

3. When booting a computer, you hear one beep followed by three, four, or five beeps during POST. What has most likely happened?

   A. The processor has overheated.

   B. There is a RAM error.

   C. The embedded keyboard or video controller failed.

   D. There is a serious problem with the motherboard's system bus, timer, BIOS setup chip, or DMA.

   220-702 A+ Objective 2.4, "Evaluate and resolve common issues"

4. You hear one beep during POST, but the screen remains blank. Where does the problem most likely reside?

   A. The power supply

   B. The video card

   C. The monitor or monitor cable

   D. The operating system

   220-702 A+ Objective 2.4, "Evaluate and resolve common issues"

2

5. When booting a computer, you see the following error: "MULTI_BIT_ECC_ERROR". What does this mean?

   A. There is a memory failure; replace the RAM.

   B. The OS bootloader could not be found; examine the hard drive for errors.

   C. BIOS setup memory has given an error; try flashing the BIOS.

   D. The processor overheated.

   220-702 A+ Objective 2.4, "Evaluate and resolve common issues"

6. When booting a computer, you see the following error: "Missing BOOTMGR". What does this mean?

   A. There is a memory failure; replace the RAM.

   B. The OS bootloader could not be found; examine the hard drive for errors.

   C. BIOS setup memory has given an error; try flashing the BIOS.

   D. The processor overheated.

   220-702 A+ Objective 2.4, "Evaluate and resolve common issues"

7. When booting a computer, you see the following error: "CMOS_CHECKSUM_ERROR". What does this mean?

   A. There is a memory failure; replace the RAM.

   B. The OS bootloader could not be found; examine the hard drive for errors.

   C. BIOS setup memory has given an error; try flashing the BIOS.

   D. The processor overheated.

   220-702 A+ Objective 2.4, "Evaluate and resolve common issues"

8. You have been asked to examine a motherboard for signs of a hardware problem. A bad capacitor can be identified by which of the following features?

   A. Bulging heads

   B. Discoloration

   C. Crusty corrosion at the base

   D. All of the above

   220-702 A+ Objective 2.4, "Evaluate and resolve common issues"

9. A device is giving you problems, and you want to uninstall and reinstall it. Where in Windows would you do this?

   A. The Device Manager

   B. The My Computer window

   C. BIOS setup

   D. The manufacturer's Web page

   220-702 A+ Objective 2.3, "Select and use system utilities/tools and evaluate the results"

10. A computer has a user profile namespace for a user named Fred. Where is it located in Windows Vista?

A. C:\Users\Fred

B. C:\Fred

C. C:\Documents and Settings\Fred

D. C:\Windows\Profiles\Fred

220-702 A+ Objective 2.2, "Differentiate between Windows operating system directory structures"

11. A computer has a user profile namespace for a user named Fred. Where is it located in Windows XP?

A. C:\Users\Fred

B. C:\Fred

C. C:\Documents and Settings\Fred

D. C:\Windows\Profiles\Fred

220-702 A+ Objective 2.2, "Differentiate between Windows operating system directory structures"

12. You are explaining the default folders in Windows to a client. In 32-bit versions of Windows, where are program files stored?

A. C:\Program Files

B. C:\Program Files (x32)

C. C:\Program Files (x64)

D. C:\Program Files (x86)

220-702 A+ Objective 2.2, "Differentiate between Windows operating system directory structures"

13. You are explaining the default folders in Windows to a client. In 64-bit versions of Windows, where are 32-bit program files stored?

A. C:\Program Files

B. C:\Program Files (x32)

C. C:\Program Files (x64)

D. C:\Program Files (x86)

220-702 A+ Objective 2.2, "Differentiate between Windows operating system directory structures"

2

14. You are explaining the default folders in Windows to a client. In 64-bit versions of Windows, where are 64-bit program files stored?

    A. C:\Program Files

    B. C:\Program Files (x32)

    C. C:\Program Files (x64)

    D. C:\Program Files (x86)

    220-702 A+ Objective 2.2, "Differentiate between Windows operating system directory structures"

15. A client would like to know more about where Internet Explorer stores personal information. In Windows Vista, where are Internet Explorer's cookies, cache, and history stored?

    A. C:\Users\username\AppData\Local\Microsoft\Windows\Temporary Internet Files

    B. C:\Program Files\Internet Explorer\Temporary Internet Files

    C. C:\Documents and Settings\username\Local Settings\Temporary Internet Files

    D. C:\Windows\Temp\username\Microsoft\Internet Explorer\Temporary Internet Files

    220-702 A+ Objective 2.2, "Differentiate between Windows operating system directory structures"

16. A client would like to know more about where Internet Explorer stores personal information. In Windows XP, where are Internet Explorer's cookies, cache, and history stored?

    A. C:\Users\username\AppData\Local\Microsoft\Windows\Temporary Internet Files

    B. C:\Program Files\Internet Explorer\Temporary Internet Files

    C. C:\Documents and Settings\username\Local Settings\Temporary Internet Files

    D. C:\Windows\Temp\username\Microsoft\Internet Explorer\Temporary Internet Files

    220-702 A+ Objective 2.2, "Differentiate between Windows operating system directory structures"

17. You are helping a client over the phone. You explain that to obtain a window with a command-line interface, you should enter what in the Vista Start Search or XP Run box?

    A. cli.exe

    B. msinfo32.exe

    C. cmd.exe

    D. command prompt

    220-702 A+ Objective 2.1, "Select the appropriate commands and options to troubleshoot and resolve problems"

18. A client asks you to explain basic backup commands. To copy only those files that have changed since the last backup, what command should be used?

    A. copy /a

    B. copy /v

    C. copy /y

    D. xcopy /d

    220-702 A+ Objective 2.1, "Select the appropriate commands and options to troubleshoot and resolve problems"

19. A client asks you to explain basic directory commands. To create a subdirectory under the current directory, which command should you use?

    A. CD

    B. MD

    C. RD

    D. makedir

    220-702 A+ Objective 2.1, "Select the appropriate commands and options to troubleshoot and resolve problems"

20. You are instructing a client on basic system commands. To check for bad sectors on a drive using the chkdsk command, what switch should be added?

    A. /f

    B. /r

    C. /s

    D. /d

    220-702 A+ Objective 2.1, "Select the appropriate commands and options to troubleshoot and resolve problems"

21. You are performing basic maintenance on a computer. What does the defrag command do?

    A. Removes temporary files left by computer games

    B. Examines a disk for files written in noncontiguous clusters and rewrites those files to contiguous clusters

    C. Repairs worn-out sector markings on magnetic disks such as hard drives

    D. All of the above

    220-702 A+ Objective 2.3, "Select and use system utilities/tools and evaluate the results"

22. You are performing basic maintenance on a computer. How often should a drive be defragmented?

    A. Daily

    B. Weekly

    C. Monthly

    D. Yearly

    220-702 A+ Objective 2.3, "Select and use system utilities/tools and evaluate the results"

23. You would like to quickly create a batch file at the command line. What is the appropriate command?

    A. bat

    B. edit

    C. format

    D. batch

    220-702 A+ Objective 2.1, "Select the appropriate commands and options to troubleshoot and resolve problems"

2

24. You would like to create and save a batch file. Which of these programs is appropriate for creating or editing a batch file?

    A. Microsoft Word

    B. WordPerfect

    C. Notepad

    D. Windows Explorer

    220-702 A+ Objective 2.1, "Select the appropriate commands and options to troubleshoot and resolve problems"

25. You need to install a file system on a volume or logical drive. How can you do this?

    A. Using Windows Disk Management

    B. Using Windows Explorer

    C. Using the format command at the command prompt

    D. All of the above

    220-702 A+ Objective 2.3, "Select and use system utilities/tools and evaluate the results"

26. Suppose you want to configure a system such that all user data resides on another volume or drive than the Windows volume. How can you achieve this?

    A. Make C:\Users the mount point for a mounted drive.

    B. Format a second volume as exFAT, with a volume label of "Users."

    C. You can only configure this as an option while installing Windows.

    D. You cannot do this.

    220-702 A+ Objective 2.3, "Select and use system utilities/tools and evaluate the results"

27. You are installing Windows on a system on which you want to use Windows dynamic disks. What version of Windows does *not* support dynamic disks?

    A. Windows Vista Home

    B. Windows XP Professional

    C. Windows Vista Business

    D. Windows Vista Enterprise

    220-702 A+ Objective 2.3, "Select and use system utilities/tools and evaluate the results"

28. You are preparing to install Windows and configure dynamic disks. What function of a dynamic disk is available in Windows XP but not in Windows Vista?

    A. Simple dynamic volumes

    B. Spanning

    C. Striping or RAID 0

    D. Mirroring or RAID 1

    220-702 A+ Objective 2.3, "Select and use system utilities/tools and evaluate the results"

29. You are partitioning a basic disk that you might one day want to convert to a dynamic disk. What step should you take to make this conversion easier?

    A. Use only basic partitions, not logical partitions.

    B. Format the disk as FAT32.

    C. Leave 1 MB of space at the end of the drive unpartitioned.

    D. Leave 1 MB of space at the beginning of the drive unpartitioned.

    220-702 A+ Objective 2.3, "Select and use system utilities/tools and evaluate the results"

30. You are examining the statuses of volumes in the Disk Manager. You see one volume is marked as Active. What does this mean?

    A. The volume is formatted with a file system, and the file system is working without errors.

    B. The disk has been sensed by Windows and can be accessed by either reading or writing to the disk.

    C. It is the volume that startup BIOS looks to in order to load an OS, and the OS boot record is located at the beginning of this partition.

    D. The volume is being formatted.

    220-702 A+ Objective 2.3, "Select and use system utilities/tools and evaluate the results"

31. You are examining the statuses of volumes in the Disk Manager. You see one volume is marked as Healthy. What does this mean?

    A. The volume is formatted with a file system, and the file system is working without errors.

    B. The disk has been sensed by Windows and can be accessed by either reading or writing to the disk.

    C. It is the volume that startup BIOS looks to in order to load an OS, and the OS boot record is located at the beginning of this partition.

    D. The volume is being formatted.

    220-702 A+ Objective 2.3, "Select and use system utilities/tools and evaluate the results"

32. You are examining the statuses of volumes in the Disk Manager. You see one volume is marked as Online. What does this mean?

    A. The volume is formatted with a file system, and the file system is working without errors.

    B. The disk has been sensed by Windows and can be accessed by either reading or writing to the disk.

    C. It is the volume that startup BIOS looks to in order to load an OS, and the OS boot record is located at the beginning of this partition.

    D. The volume is being formatted.

    220-702 A+ Objective 2.3, "Select and use system utilities/tools and evaluate the results"

2

33. You are examining the statuses of volumes in the Disk Manager. You see one disk is marked as Foreign drive. What does this mean?

    A. The files on the drive are in a different language or different encoding than this computer.

    B. Windows does not recognize the file system on this drive.

    C. This is a dynamic disk configured on another computer, and it must be imported.

    D. This is a dynamic disk that has become corrupted or is unavailable due to a hardware problem.

    220-702 A+ Objective 2.3 "Select and use system utilities/tools and evaluate the results"

34. You are planning a system that will employ RAID. Generally speaking, is it better to use hardware RAID or Windows software RAID?

    A. Hardware RAID, because Windows cannot be installed on a software RAID volume

    B. Hardware RAID, because it is more stable

    C. Both of the above

    D. Software RAID

    220-702 A+ Objective 2.3, "Select and use system utilities/tools and evaluate the results"

35. You need to support a user who wants to work in another language. Language packs can be installed using Windows Update only under what condition?

    A. It is one of a few common languages supported by Microsoft.

    B. The system is running Windows Vista Ultimate Edition.

    C. The system is running Windows Vista International Edition.

    D. There are no conditions other than being connected to the Internet.

    220-702 A+ Objective 2.3, "Select and use system utilities/tools and evaluate the results"

36. You are trying to clean up a slow Windows Vista system and discover that the 75 GB hard drive has only 5 GB of free space. The entire drive is taken up by drive C. What is the best way to free up some space?

    A. Compress the entire hard drive.

    B. Move the \Program Files folder to an external hard drive.

    C. Delete the Windows.old folder.

    D. Reduce the size of the paging file.

    220-702 A+ Objective 2.4, "Evaluate and resolve common issues"

37. A client asks you to explain how to protect data on a computer. What is the best first step to protect important data on a hard drive?

    A. Use dynamic disks to set up a striped volume so that the data has redundancy.

    B. Back up the data to another medium.

    C. Compress the folder that holds the data.

    D. Put password protection on the data folder.

    220-702 A+ Objective 2.4, "Evaluate and resolve common issues"

38. You are asked to assess the performance of a client's computer. What is the first step in optimizing a system's performance?

A. Perform routine maintenance.

B. Check if the hardware can support the OS.

C. Check for performance warnings.

D. Disable various Vista enhancements.

220-702 A+ Objective 2.4, "Evaluate and resolve common issues"

39. You are asked to assess the performance of a client's computer. What tool could be used to measure the overall performance of a system and identify performance bottlenecks for Windows Vista?

A. Vista Upgrade Advisor

B. Device Manager

C. System Information Utility

D. Windows Experience Index

220-702 A+ Objective 2.3, "Select and use system utilities/tools and evaluate the results"

40. You are asked to assess the performance of a client's computer. Where can you see performance warnings Windows Vista has identified with a running system?

A. Advanced Tools in the Windows Experience Index

B. System Information Utility

C. System Log in the Event Viewer

D. All of the above

220-702 A+ Objective 2.3, "Select and use system utilities/tools and evaluate the results"

41. You are asked to assess the performance of a client's computer. Which utility would you open to see a graph of system stability over time, along with indications of when various events such as software installations took place?

A. Windows Experience Index

B. System Log in the Event Viewer

C. Reliability Monitor in the Reliability and Performance Monitor

D. None of the above

220-702 A+ Objective 2.3, "Select and use system utilities/tools and evaluate the results"

42. You notice that your computer's performance slows after the system has been up and running without a restart for some time. What should you suspect as a culprit?

A. Overheating

B. File system fragmentation

C. A memory leak in a running application

D. Too many startup programs

220-702 A+ Objective 2.3, "Select and use system utilities/tools and evaluate the results"

2

43. You are asked to assess the performance of a client's computer. You know that using Vista ReadyBoost will result in the greatest performance increase in which circumstance?

    A. The hard drive is nearly full.

    B. The hard drive's rotation speed is slow.

    C. The system has a slow memory speed.

    D. The system has little RAM.

    220-702 A+ Objective 2.3, "Select and use system utilities/tools and evaluate the results"

44. You would like to set up a client's Windows XP machine to automatically defragment the disk weekly at a given time. How can this be done?

    A. Use the Disk Defragmenter tool's options to set it to run at a given time every week.

    B. Use the Task Scheduler to schedule Disk Defragmenter to run weekly.

    C. From the Calendar application, create a recurring event to run Disk Defragmenter.

    D. All of the above.

    220-702 A+ Objective 2.3, "Select and use system utilities/tools and evaluate the results"

45. You are asked to assess the performance of a client's computer. When trying to improve Windows performance, what should you try disabling first?

    A. Antivirus software, which runs in the background and takes up resources

    B. The Vista Aero interface ("Aero Glass")

    C. Microsoft services

    D. The Vista UAC box

    220-702 A+ Objective 2.4, "Evaluate and resolve common issues"

46. Suppose the uninstall routine for a program you need to uninstall fails and you must manually delete the program files. What else do you need to do to fully uninstall the program?

    A. Delete the registry entries pertaining to the program.

    B. Remove the program from the All Programs menu.

    C. Restart and fix any errors.

    D. All of the above.

    220-702 A+ Objective 2.4, "Evaluate and resolve common issues"

47. You need to stop a process that has hung. Which tool lets you view services and other running programs, CPU and memory performance, network activity, and user activity, and allows you to terminate processes?

    A. Event Viewer (Eventvwr.msc)

    B. Services Console (Services.msc)

    C. Msconfig (Msconfig.exe)

    D. Task Manager (Taskmgr.exe)

    220-702 A+ Objective 2.3, "Select and use system utilities/tools and evaluate the results"

48. You need to temporarily disable startup processes to test for performance improvement. What tool should you use?

A. Event Viewer (Eventvwr.msc)

B. Services console (Services.msc)

C. Msconfig (Msconfig.exe)

D. Task Manager (Taskmgr.exe)

220-702 A+ Objective 2.3, "Select and use system utilities/tools and evaluate the results"

49. You need to find a startup program causing a problem. What tool should you use?

A. Event Viewer (Eventvwr.msc)

B. Services console (Services.msc)

C. Msconfig (Msconfig.exe)

D. Task Manager (Taskmgr.exe)

220-702 A+ Objective 2.3, "Select and use system utilities/tools and evaluate the results"

50. You need to control when and if a service starts. What tool should you use?

A. Event Viewer (Eventvwr.msc)

B. Services console (Services.msc)

C. Msconfig (Msconfig.exe)

D. Task Manager (Taskmgr.exe)

220-702 A+ Objective 2.3, "Select and use system utilities/tools and evaluate the results"

51. You are evaluating performance problems in a client's system, and you observe that performance improves when the system is booted in Safe Mode. What can you conclude?

A. Nonessential startup programs are slowing down the system when Windows starts normally.

B. Something unsafe is being started when Windows starts normally.

C. The problem is with a hardware device, critical driver, or Windows component.

D. Antivirus software is harming the system's performance.

220-702 A+ Objective 2.4, "Evaluate and resolve common issues"

52. You are evaluating performance problems in a client's system, and you observe that performance does *not* improve when the system is booted in Safe Mode. What can you conclude?

A. Nonessential startup programs are slowing down the system when Windows starts normally.

B. Something unsafe is being started when Windows starts normally.

C. The problem is with a hardware device, critical driver, or Windows component.

D. Antivirus software is harming the system's performance.

220-702 A+ Objective 2.4, "Evaluate and resolve common issues"

2

53. You are evaluating performance problems in a client's system. Which value in the Task Manager's Processes tab can indicate a memory leak?

   A. Memory Private Working Set

   B. Handles

   C. Threads

   D. All of the above

   220-702 A+ Objective 2.3, "Select and use system utilities/tools and evaluate the results"

54. You are evaluating performance problems in a client's system. When cleaning up the startup process, what should you do first?

   A. Run Msconfig to see what processes are started.

   B. If an error message is displayed when you start Windows, investigate the message.

   C. After you have launched several applications, use Task Manager to view a list of running tasks.

   D. Run the Defrag utility to optimize the hard drive.

   220-702 A+ Objective 2.4, "Evaluate and resolve common issues"

55. You are troubleshooting an issue on a client's computer. What command/tool can you run to verify and replace system files?

   A. System Restore

   B. System File Checker

   C. Services Console

   D. Msconfig

   220-702 A+ Objective 2.3, "Select and use system utilities/tools and evaluate the results"

56. You are troubleshooting an issue on a client's computer. When faced with a problem with a device driver or service, what should be the first step?

   A. Update the device drivers.

   B. Update Windows.

   C. Reboot.

   D. Move the device to a different computer.

   220-702 A+ Objective 2.4, "Evaluate and resolve common issues"

57. You are troubleshooting an issue on a client's computer. After making a change to a system you are trying to fix, what should you do?

   A. Back up the system.

   B. Restart the system.

   C. Check the log files and Event Viewer to see if the change fixed the problem.

   D. All of the above.

   220-702 A+ Objective 2.4, "Evaluate and resolve common issues"

58. You have been asked to find the source of a problem with an application. What should be your first step?

    A. Ask the user to reproduce the problem while you watch.

    B. Try a reboot.

    C. Allow Windows to provide a solution

    D. Interview the user and back up data.

    220-702 A+ Objective 2.4, "Evaluate and resolve common issues"

59. A user tells you she started having problems with an application about three days ago. You have already rebooted, downloaded and installed updates to Windows and the application, restored the default application settings, and uninstalled and reinstalled the application, to no avail. What might be an appropriate next step?

    A. Run the application as an administrator.

    B. Use System Restore to restore to a point just before the problem started.

    C. Try the application on another computer.

    D. Edit the registry.

    220-702 A+ Objective 2.4, "Evaluate and resolve common issues"

60. You are diagnosing a customer's problems with an application. You find that the application works in Safe Mode with Networking, but not normally. What can you conclude?

    A. The application has been infected with a virus.

    B. The application requires an Internet connection to function correctly.

    C. The problem is not actually with the application, but with the operating system, device drivers, or another conflicting application.

    D. You cannot actually conclude anything—more information is needed.

    220-702 A+ Objective 2.4, "Evaluate and resolve common issues"

61. You are diagnosing a computer that is having problems booting. No error messages are showing up in BIOS, but problems are occurring before the Microsoft progress bar appears. What kind of general problem is this?

    A. Corrupt or missing system files or hardware

    B. Problems with user mode services or drivers

    C. Problems caused by startup scripts

    D. Problems caused by applications

    220-702 A+ Objective 2.4, "Evaluate and resolve common issues"

2

62. You are diagnosing a computer that is having problems booting. No error messages are showing up in BIOS, but problems are occurring before the Microsoft progress bar appears. What are the best Vista tools for such problems?

    A. Msconfig, Safe Mode

    B. Last Known Good Configuration, Device Manager

    C. Startup Repair, System Restore

    D. Software Explorer, Reliability and Performance Monitor

    220-702 A+ Objective 2.4, "Evaluate and resolve common issues"

63. You are diagnosing a computer that is having problems booting. The Microsoft progress bar appears, but the problem is cropping up before the logon screen appears. What kind of general problem is this?

    A. Corrupt or missing system files or hardware

    B. Problems with user mode services or drivers

    C. Problems caused by startup scripts

    D. Problems caused by applications

    220-702 Objective 2.4, "Evaluate and resolve common issues"

64. You are diagnosing a computer that is having problems booting: the Microsoft progress bar appears, but the problem crops up before the logon screen appears. What are the best Vista tools for such problems?

    A. Msconfig, Safe Mode

    B. Last Known Good Configuration, Device Manager

    C. Startup Repair, System Restore

    D. All of the above

    220-702 A+ Objective 2.4, "Evaluate and resolve common issues"

65. You are diagnosing a problem with Vista that occurs after the logon screen appears. What kind of general problem is this?

    A. Corrupt or missing system files or hardware

    B. Problems with user mode services or drivers

    C. Problems caused by startup scripts or applications

    D. Incorrect drivers

    220-702 A+ Objective 2.4, "Evaluate and resolve common issues"

66. You are diagnosing a problem with Vista that occurs after the logon screen appears. What are the best Vista tools for such problems?

    A. Msconfig, Safe Mode

    B. Last Known Good Configuration, Device Manager

    C. Startup Repair, System Restore

    D. All of the above

    220-702 A+ Objective 2.4, "Evaluate and resolve common issues"

67. During bootup, BIOS reports an error: "No boot device available". What does this indicate?
   A. BIOS could not find a hard drive, perhaps due to a physical problem with the drive, cable, power, or motherboard.
   B. BIOS was able to find the hard drive, but it couldn't read what was written on the drive or could not find what it was looking for.
   C. Vista's system files or drivers are corrupted.
   D. POST has failed.
   220-702 A+ Objective 2.4, "Evaluate and resolve common issues"

68. During bootup, BIOS reports an error: "Inaccessible boot device". What does this indicate?
   A. BIOS could not find a hard drive, perhaps due to a physical problem with the drive, cable, power, or motherboard.
   B. BIOS was able to find the hard drive, but it couldn't read what was written on the drive or could not find what it was looking for.
   C. Vista's system files or drivers are corrupted.
   D. POST has failed.
   220-702 A+ Objective 2.4, "Evaluate and resolve common issues"

69. During bootup, BIOS reports an error: "bootmgr is missing". What does this indicate?
   A. BIOS could not find a hard drive, perhaps due to a physical problem with the drive, cable, power, or motherboard.
   B. BIOS was able to find the hard drive, but it couldn't read what was written on the drive or could not find what it was looking for.
   C. Vista's system files or drivers are corrupted.
   D. POST has failed.
   220-702 A+ Objective 2.4, "Evaluate and resolve common issues"

70. During bootup, BIOS reports an error: "Disk boot failure, insert system disk and press enter." You confirm that the BIOS boot sequence is set to boot first off the internal hard drive. What should your next course of action be?
   A. Set BIOS setup to boot off the DVD drive, and then insert and boot from the Windows Vista setup DVD.
   B. Examine the computer for a physical problem with the hard drive, taking the appropriate precautions.
   C. Reformat the hard drive.
   D. Check BIOS setup to verify that BIOS detected the drive correctly.
   220-702 A+ Objective 2.4, "Evaluate and resolve common issues"

2

71. What is a good first step in troubleshooting a system that runs into problems after the Microsoft progress bar has appeared before the logon screen?

    A. Run Startup Repair from the Windows Recovery Environment menu.

    B. Boot to the Advanced Boot Options menu and select Enable Boot Logging.

    C. Run System Restore from the Windows Recovery Environment.

    D. Replace the hard drive.

    220-702 A+ Objective 2.4, "Evaluate and resolve common issues"

72. You are trying to solve a problem with a device or its drivers. Which of the following tools is *not* likely to be helpful?

    A. System Restore

    B. Safe Mode

    C. Device Manager

    D. Task Manager

    220-702 A+ Objective 2.3, "Select and use system utilities/tools and evaluate the results"

73. You are trying to identify the device that is causing a problem on a system. Which of the following tools is *not* likely to be helpful?

    A. Vista Problem Reports and Solutions tool

    B. Startup Repair

    C. Reliability and Performance Monitor

    D. Event Viewer

    220-702 A+ Objective 2.3, "Select and use system utilities/tools and evaluate the results"

74. You are trying to fix a problem with an application. Which of the following tools is *not* likely to be helpful?

    A. Task Manager

    B. System File Checker

    C. Vista Problem Reports and Solutions

    D. Windows updates

    220-702 A+ Objective 2.3, "Select and use system utilities/tools and evaluate the results"

75. You are troubleshooting a failed boot. Which of the following tools and techniques is *not* likely to be helpful?

    A. Device Manager

    B. Safe Mode

    C. Last Known Good Configuration

    D. Startup Repair

    220-702 A+ Objective 2.3, "Select and use system utilities/tools and evaluate the results"

76. You are installing the hard drive from a machine that won't boot into another machine as a second hard drive. What is the most compelling reason to do this?

    A. To test whether the working machine can boot off the drive

    B. To test whether the troubled machine will boot without it

    C. To recover the data on the drive

    D. To protect the hard drive from further damage due to a bad power supply or motherboard

    220-702 A+ Objective 2.4, "Evaluate and resolve common issues"

77. You are reviewing some commands before evaluating a system. What is the command "mdsched.exe" used for?

    A. Scheduling directory creation

    B. Testing memory

    C. Altering the priority of tasks

    D. Setting up regular maintenance tasks such as defragmenting disks

    220-702 A+ Objective 2.1, "Select the appropriate commands and options to troubleshoot and resolve problems"

78. You would like to uninstall a USB device. What Windows Vista tool can you use to do this?

    A. Device Manager

    B. System Restore

    C. Windows Update

    D. System Information

    220-702 A+ Objective 2.3, "Select and use system utilities/tools and evaluate the results"

79. You would like to uninstall a FireWire device. What Windows XP tool can you use to do this?

    A. Device Manager

    B. System Restore

    C. Windows Update

    D. System Information

    220-702 A+ Objective 2.3, "Select and use system utilities/tools and evaluate the results"

80. You would like to uninstall a network card. What Windows tool can you use to do this?

    A. Device Manager

    B. System Restore

    C. Windows Update

    D. System Information

    220-702 A+ Objective 2.3, "Select and use system utilities/tools and evaluate the results"

2

81. What Windows tool can you use to restore the Windows system to a previous point in time before a device was installed?

    A. Device Manager

    B. System Restore

    C. Windows Update

    D. System Information

    220-702 A+ Objective 2.3, "Select and use system utilities/tools and evaluate the results"

82. You would like to update your video drivers. What Windows tool can you use to do this?

    A. Device Manager

    B. System Restore

    C. Windows Update

    D. System Information

    220-702 A+ Objective 2.3, "Select and use system utilities/tools and evaluate the results"

83. Windows Vista refuses to start and the error message says something about the WinLoad program file being missing. What is the best way to fix the problem?

    A. Boot from the Vista DVD and use the command prompt window to copy the WinLoad file from a working PC to this PC.

    B. Boot from the Vista DVD and use the Startup Repair tool.

    C. Use the latest Complete PC backup to restore the system.

    D. Boot into Safe Mode and restore the program from backup.

    220-702 A+ Objective 2.4, "Evaluate and resolve common issues"

84. You tried to use the Automated System Recovery to restore a failed Windows XP system. The process failed with errors, but there is an extremely important data file on the hard drive that you need to recover. The hard drive is using the NTFS file system. What do you do?

    A. Most likely the file is toast. The ASR process probably destroyed the file if it was not already destroyed.

    B. Boot to the Recovery Console using the Windows XP setup CD and attempt to recover the file.

    C. Reinstall Windows XP and then recover the file.

    D. Boot to the Advanced Options menu and use Safe Mode to recover the file.

    220-702 A+ Objective 2.4, "Evaluate and resolve common issues"

85. You suspect that a user's settings are causing a problem at login. What file contains user settings that are copied to the registry when the user logs in?

    A. C:\Users\UserName\Ntuser.dat

    B. C:\Windows\system32\config\UserName\Ntuser.dat

    C. C:\Users\UserName\AppData\Microsoft\regdat.cfg

    D. All of the above

    220-702 A+ Objective 2.2, "Differentiate between Windows operating system directory structures"

86. You need to run privileged commands from the command-line interface in Vista. How is this done?

    A. Enter cmd+.exe in the Vista Start Search box.

    B. Start the CLI like usual, and then enter the su command.

    C. Click Start, All Programs, Accessories, and then right-click Command Prompt to select Run as administrator.

    D. All of the above

    220-702 A+ Objective 2.1, "Select the appropriate commands and options to troubleshoot and resolve problems"

87. You are creating a file at the command line. Which of the following is *not* a valid filename?

    A. ~myfile.txt

    B. my_file.txt

    C. My File.txt

    D. what's the deal?.txt

    220-702 A+ Objective 2.1, "Select the appropriate commands and options to troubleshoot and resolve problems"

88. You have changed the network a computer is using or moved the computer to a different network. What command can you use to release and renew the computer's network address?

    A. Msconfig

    B. Ntbackup

    C. Ipconfig

    D. Nslookup

    220-702 A+ Objective 2.1, "Select the appropriate commands and options to troubleshoot and resolve problems"

89. You are creating a file at the command line. Which of the following is *not* a valid filename?

    A. How to make big $$$!.doc

    B. Amy & Brad's # @home.doc

    C. ★★★important!★★★.doc

    D. my stuff (Jan-Dec 2009).doc

    220-702 A+ Objective 2.1, "Select the appropriate commands and options to troubleshoot and resolve problems"

90. You need to set up a network drive, but you are having difficulty using the graphical methods. Which type of Net command can you use to map a network drive?

    A. Net use

    B. Net config

    C. Net file

    D. None of the above

    220-702 A+ Objective 2.1, "Select the appropriate commands and options to troubleshoot and resolve problems"

2

91. A Vista user has a number of files that are to be shared with other members of her team. Where does Microsoft encourage the user to store such files?

    A. C:\Users\Public

    B. C:\Users\Team

    C. C:\Public

    D. C:\Shared

    220-702 A+ Objective 2.2, "Differentiate between Windows operating system directory structures"

92. You need to edit the registry. Where is it stored?

    A. C:\Windows\Registry

    B. C:\Windows\system32\config

    C. C:\Users\username\Ntuser

    D. C:\Windows\System\Library\

    220-702 A+ Objective 2.2, "Differentiate between Windows operating system directory structures"

93. You are working at the command prompt and need to see a list of what is in the current folder. What is the command to use?

    A. fldr

    B. ls

    C. dir

    D. list

    220-702 A+ Objective 2.1, "Select the appropriate commands and options to troubleshoot and resolve problems"

94. You are working at the command prompt and need to delete a file. What is the command to use?

    A. rm

    B. del

    C. erase

    D. either B or C

    220-702 A+ Objective 2.1, "Select the appropriate commands and options to troubleshoot and resolve problems"

95. You are preparing to partition a hard drive. How many primary partitions may a drive have under Windows?

    A. One

    B. Up to three

    C. Up to four

    D. Limited only by block size and drive capacity

    220-702 A+ Objective 2.3, "Select and use system utilities/tools and evaluate the results"

96. You are verifying and cleaning out startup programs for a user. Where does Windows Vista store shortcuts to programs to start up for the user UserName?

A. C:\Windows\StartupItems\UserName

B. C:\Users\UserName\StartupItems

C. C:\Users\UserName\AppData\Roaming\Microsoft\Windows\Start Menu\Programs\Startup

D. C:\Users\UserName\Windows\system32\Start Menu\Items\Startup

220-702 A+ Objective 2.2, "Differentiate between Windows operating system directory structures"

97. You are advising a client about which version of Windows to purchase. Which version of Windows does *not* include Complete PC Backup?

A. Vista Home

B. Vista Business

C. Vista Ultimate

D. Vista Enterprise

220-702 A+ Objective 2.2, "Differentiate between Windows operating system directory structures"

98. As routine maintenance on client computers, at least what percentage of drive C should you try to keep free?

A. 5%

B. 10%

C. 15%

D. 20%

220-702 A+ Objective 2.4, "Evaluate and resolve common issues"

99. You want to back up the system state of a Windows XP machine before making changes to the registry. What tool do you use?

A. Xpbackup

B. Ntbackup

C. System Restore

D. Complete PC Backup

220-702 A+ Objective 2.4, "Evaluate and resolve common issues"

100. You are shopping for a flash device to improve system performance. What are the minimum requirements for a flash device to be used with ReadyBoost?

A. 128 MB of free space, 1 MB/s throughput

B. 256 MB of free space, 2 MB/s throughput

C. 1 GB of free space, 2.5 MB/s throughput

D. 4 GB of free space, 2.5 MB/s throughput

220-702 A+ Objective 2.4, "Evaluate and resolve common issues"

2

101. You are trying to squeeze every bit of performance out of a system for a demanding user on a limited hardware budget. You are considering moving the Pagefile.sys to another disk. In what circumstance might this yield a benefit?

    A. When the new location is on a faster disk than the old location

    B. When the new location has plenty of space

    C. Both of the above

    D. Never

    220-702 A+ Objective 2.4, "Evaluate and resolve common issues"

102. To clear out a bit of disk space, you want to delete the client side cache folder. Where is that located?

    A. C:\Windows\CSC

    B. C:\Users\UserName\Temporary\CSC

    C. C:\Users\UserName\AppData\Microsoft\CSC

    D. C:\Windows\system32\caches\CSC

    220-702 A+ Objective 2.2, "Differentiate between Windows operating system directory structures"

3.0

NETWORKING

1. You are installing a cable modem in a client's home. How should you select where to put the cable modem?

   A. Placing the modem right next to the computer that will connect to the modem is best, to keep the connection over a short distance.

   B. Most clients prefer the cable modem to be out of sight, for example, such as in a closet.

   C. Use the jack that connects directly to the point where the cable comes into the house, with no splitters between the jack and entrance point.

   D. The cable modem must be close to the TV and VCR/cable box.

   220-702 A+ Objective 3.2, "Install and configure a small home office (SOHO) network"

2. You are installing a cable modem in a client's home. In the cable modem documentation, the cable used to connect the cable modem to the PC may be referred to as which of the following?

   A. Ethernet cable

   B. Patch cable

   C. USB cable

   D. All of the above

   220-702 A+ Objective 3.2, "Install and configure a small home office (SOHO) network"

3. You are installing a cable modem in a client's home. What piece of information does the cable company need to know about the client's cable modem?

   A. Serial number

   B. MAC address

   C. Manufacturer and model number

   D. LAN IP address

   220-702 A+ Objective 3.2, "Install and configure a small home office (SOHO) network"

4. You are discussing the differences between a DSL and cable modem with a colleague. Compared to a cable modem, installing a DSL connection requires what additional piece of hardware (in addition to the DSL modem)?

   A. A telephone filter on every phone jack in the house that is being used

   B. A USB terminator

   C. A dedicated DSL network card in the PC

   D. A DSL converter box between the DSL modem and the wall jack

   220-702 A+ Objective 3.2, "Install and configure a small home office (SOHO) network"

3

5. You are configuring an on-demand broadband connection that requires authentication each time you connect. Such a connection is managed by what protocol?

   A. USB

   B. Ethernet

   C. Point-to-Point over Ethernet (PPPoE)

   D. TCP/IP

   220-702 Objective 3.2, "Install and configure a small home office (SOHO) network"

6. A client is asking you about appropriate firewalls for a small network. What type of firewall is most appropriate for a small office network with three PCs sharing a broadband connection to the Internet?

   A. Software firewall

   B. Hardware firewall

   C. No firewall is needed

   D. ISDN

   220-702 A+ Objective 3.2, "Install and configure a small home office (SOHO) network"

7. You are discussing network protection with a client. Which of the following can filter data packets and ports and block certain Internet activity?

   A. A modern wireless router

   B. Windows Firewall

   C. McAfee VirusScan Plus

   D. All of the above

   220-702 A+ Objective 3.2, "Install and configure a small home office (SOHO) network"

8. You are learning about Vista's Windows Firewall. What option offers the highest level of protection?

   A. Public profile.

   B. Private profile.

   C. Domain profile.

   D. All profiles provide the same level of protection.

   220-702 A+ Objective 3.2, "Install and configure a small home office network"

9. You are learning about Vista's Windows Firewall. What option offers the least protection?

   A. Public profile.

   B. Private profile.

   C. Domain profile.

   D. All profiles provide the same level of protection.

   220-702 A+ Objective 3.2, "Install and configure a small home office (SOHO) network"

10. You are taking Ethernet cables with you for client installations. What is the maximum recommended length for an Ethernet cable?

   A. 1000 meters

   B. 100 meters

   C. 10 meters

   D. 1 meter

   220-702 A+ Objective 3.2, "Install and configure a small home office (SOHO) network"

11. A client asks you about the role of an Ethernet switch in a SOHO network. How can you respond?

   A. To connect two or more computers by way of Ethernet cables

   B. To turn the Ethernet network connections on or off

   C. To convert data from the form used on the internal LAN to one suitable for transmission onto the Internet

   D. To provide an Internet connection via cable, DSL, or dial-up

   220-702 A+ Objective 3.2, "Install and configure a small home office (SOHO) network"

12. You are installing a wireless router for a SOHO network. What is the best location for the wireless access point?

   A. At the highest point in the building

   B. As close to the cable or DSL modem as possible

   C. Near the center of the area where you want your wireless network

   D. Anywhere that is clear of walls or windows

   220-702 A+ Objective 3.2, "Install and configure a small home office (SOHO) network"

13. You are installing a wireless router for a SOHO network. What is the correct SOHO network architecture?

   A. ISP---Cable Modem---Router---Switch---Wireless access point and computers

   B. ISP---Switch---Cable Modem---Router---Wireless access point and computers

   C. ISP---Router---Cable Modem---Switch---Wireless access point and computers

   D. ISP---Cable Modem---Switch---Router---Wireless access point and computers

   220-702 A+ Objective 3.2, "Install and configure a small home office (SOHO) network"

14. You are configuring a wireless router for a small network. Once you plug in the router and sign in to the configuration utility, what is the first thing you should do?

   A. Check the Internet connection between the router and the cable or DSL modem.

   B. Check the connection between the computer and the router.

   C. Change the router's administrative password.

   D. Run through the configuration to get the wireless access correctly configured.

   220-702 A+ Objective 3.2, "Install and configure a small home office (SOHO) network"

3

15. A computer connected to your router is running a server (such as a Telnet server) and needs to be reliably available to other computers. What configuration must be set up on the router?

    A. Disable the router's firewall.

    B. Upgrade the router's firmware to allow for such a server.

    C. Plug the server's network cable into the dedicated server port on the router.

    D. Assign the server a static IP address.

    220-702 A+ Objective 3.2, "Install and configure a small home office (SOHO) network"

16. A client is having trouble with remote access to her computer network. What NAT mechanism is used to open or close certain ports so they cannot be used?

    A. Port triggering

    B. Port forwarding

    C. Port filtering

    D. DHCP

    220-702 A+ Objective 3.2, "Install and configure a small home office (SOHO) network"

17. A client is having trouble with remote access to her computer network. What NAT mechanism is used to allow traffic from the Internet on a given port pass to a given computer behind the firewall?

    A. Port triggering

    B. Port forwarding

    C. Port filtering

    D. DHCP

    220-702 Objective 3.2, "Install and configure a small home office (SOHO) network"

18. You are configuring NAT for a client's network. What NAT mechanism is used to allow inbound traffic on a given port when activated by outbound traffic on a different port?

    A. Port triggering

    B. Port forwarding

    C. Port filtering

    D. DHCP

    220-702 A+ Objective 3.2, "Install and configure a small home office (SOHO) network"

19. In addition to configuring port forwarding correctly on your router and configuring the service correctly on the server computer, what else is needed to enable reliable access to a server behind a firewall from elsewhere on the Internet?

    A. Your cable modem must be set to visibility mode.

    B. Your ISP needs to provide you with a static IP address.

    C. You must buy Internet hosting.

    D. Nothing.

    220-702 A+ Objective 3.2, "Install and configure a small home office (SOHO) network"

20. Your client has asked you to set up a restricted wireless network. What feature on a wireless access point allows you to limit access to specific computers?

A. SSID

B. WPA encryption

C. DHCP

D. MAC filtering

220-702 A+ Objective 3.2, "Install and configure a small home office (SOHO) network"

21. Your client has asked you to set up a restricted wireless network. What feature on a wireless access point allows you to limit the number of computers connected at once, without limiting access to specific computers?

A. SSID

B. WPA encryption

C. DHCP

D. MAC filtering

220-702 A+ Objective 3.2, "Install and configure a small home office (SOHO) network"

22. You would like to change the name of the wireless network your access point provides. What setting must be changed?

A. SSID

B. WPA encryption

C. DHCP

D. MAC filtering

220-702 A+ Objective 3.2, "Install and configure a small home office (SOHO) network"

23. You need some basic information about a customer's computer. What is the command to display the hardware address of the network card in Windows XP or Vista?

A. Hardaddr

B. Getmac

C. Netstat

D. Nicinfo

220-702 A+ Objective 3.1, "Troubleshoot client-side connectivity issues using appropriate tools"

24. You would like to look up information about the domain name www.microsoft.com. What command should you use?

A. Net /?

B. Netstat

C. Nslookup

D. Telnet

220-702 A+ Objective 3.1, "Troubleshoot client-side connectivity issues using appropriate tools"

3

25. You would like to see information about your current TCP/IP connections. What command should you use?

    A. Ipconfig

    B. Netstat

    C. Telnet

    D. Net /?

    220-702 A+ Objective 3.1, "Troubleshoot client-side connectivity issues using appropriate tools"

26. You would like to release and renew a computer's network address to see if this solves a networking issue. What command should you use?

    A. Nslookup

    B. Getmac

    C. Ipconfig

    D. Telnet

    220-702 A+ Objective 3.1, "Troubleshoot client-side connectivity issues using appropriate tools"

27. A client asks about the Telnet command. How can you explain the purpose of the Telnet command?

    A. Displays information about dial-up network connections

    B. Brings up a tool for configuring networking settings

    C. Allows you to communicate with another computer on the network remotely

    D. Displays the route taken from the host to a remote destination

    220-702 A+ Objective 3.1, "Troubleshoot client-side connectivity issues using appropriate tools"

28. You are trying to resolve a problem reaching a destination host such as an FTP or Web site. What tool sends a series of requests to the destination computer and displays each hop?

    A. Ping

    B. Nslookup

    C. Netstat

    D. Tracert

    220-702 A+ Objective 3, "Troubleshoot client-side connectivity issues using appropriate tools"

29. You are using Remote Desktop to assist a client. Which of the following operating systems *cannot* be accessed as the server using Remote Desktop?

    A. Windows Vista Ultimate

    B. Windows Vista Business

    C. Windows Vista Home

    D. Windows XP Professional

    220-702 Objective 3.1, "Troubleshoot client-side connectivity issues using appropriate tools"

30. A user would like you to see her computer's desktop as she sees it and even take control of her computer. What tool allows this?

    A. Remote Desktop

    B. Remote Assistance

    C. Telnet

    D. Network and Sharing Center

    220-702 A+ Objective 3.1, "Troubleshoot client-side connectivity issues using appropriate tools"

31. You are initiating a Remote Assistance session with a client. What is the best way to do this?

    A. The user saves an invitation file and then sends that file to the technician by any method.

    B. The user initiates a session by way of Windows Messenger.

    C. The user sends an email message to a corporate help desk.

    D. The technician initiates the session.

    220-702 A+ Objective 3.1, "Troubleshoot client-side connectivity issues using appropriate tools"

32. You are troubleshooting some networking problems. Where is it generally best to start?

    A. Troubleshoot hardware

    B. Troubleshoot device drivers and hardware

    C. Troubleshoot TCP/IP and shared resources

    D. Troubleshoot client/server connectivity

    220-702 A+ Objective 3.1, "Troubleshoot client-side connectivity issues using appropriate tools"

33. What is the first step in solving a problem with Windows TCP/IP configuration and connectivity?

    A. Run ipconfig /all and look for a 169.254 IP address.

    B. Ping 127.0.0.1.

    C. Run netstat.

    D. Release and renew the IP address in Network and Sharing Center or with ipconfig.

    220-702 A+ Objective 3.1, "Troubleshoot client-side connectivity issues using appropriate tools"

34. You see the IP address 127.0.0.1. What does this address refer to?

    A. Google

    B. Microsoft

    C. An automatic private IP address

    D. Your computer

    220-702 A+ Objective 3.1, "Troubleshoot client-side connectivity issues using appropriate tools"

3

35. You ping 127.0.0.1 and get an error message. What should you conclude?

    A. Microsoft's network is down.

    B. Your network's connection to the Internet is down.

    C. The problem is in the TCP/IP stack on your PC.

    D. Nothing; it should result in an error.

    220-702 A+ Objective 3.1, "Troubleshoot client-side connectivity issues using appropriate tools"

36. You are having a problem with slow network performance and suspect a process is hogging network resources. What tool can you use to try to find the culprit program?

    A. Netstat –b

    B. ping

    C. Network and Sharing Center

    D. Remote Assistance

    220-702 A+ Objective 3.1, "Troubleshoot client-side connectivity issues using appropriate tools"

37. When trying to reach a computer on the local network, you observe that the ping command is successful with the IP address of the remote computer, but not with the name of the remote computer. What does this suggest?

    A. The problem might be with the Hosts file on the local computer.

    B. The problem might be with wrong entries in the DNS servers that are used on the corporate network.

    C. Neither of the above.

    D. Both of the above.

    220-702 A+ Objective 3.1, "Troubleshoot client-side connectivity issues using appropriate tools"

38. You are setting up satellite Internet access for a client. What direction should the satellite dish face in North America?

    A. North

    B. South

    C. East

    D. West

    220-702 A+ Objective 3.2, "Install and configure a small home office (SOHO) network"

39. You are reading up on current Ethernet standards. What standard is fastest?

    A. 10BaseT

    B. 100BaseT

    C. 1000BaseT

    D. DSL

    220-702 A+ Objective 3.2, "Install and configure a small home office network"

40. You are installing a wireless access point for a customer who has some older laptops. What wireless encryption protocol is most likely to be compatible with older hardware?

    A. WPA

    B. WPA2

    C. WEP

    D. RADIUS

    220-702 A+ Objective 3.2, "Install and configure a small home office (SOHO) network"

41. You are having trouble setting up a network drive. Which type of Net command can be used to map a network drive?

    A. Net use

    B. Net view

    C. Net file

    D. Net config

    220-702 A+ Objective 3.1, "Troubleshoot client-side connectivity issues using appropriate tools"

42. A customer has asked you to configure his email client. Which of the following server addresses provided by myISP should be used for outgoing mail?

    A. imap.myISP.net

    B. pop.myISP.net

    C. smtp.myISP.net

    D. dns.myISP.net

    220-702 A+ Objective 3.1, "Troubleshoot client-side connectivity issues using appropriate tools"

43. You are having problems setting up a dial-up connection in Vista through the Dial-Up Connection dialog box. What is the first thing you should do?

    A. Reboot your PC.

    B. Check with the ISP to verify that you have the correct phone number, username, and password.

    C. Check the phone line to see if it's connected.

    D. Check the properties of the dial-up connection icon for errors.

    220-702 A+ Objective 3.1, "Troubleshoot client-side connectivity issues using appropriate tools"

3

44. You have a small home network on a DSL connection with two PCs running Vista. The two computers can connect to the Internet but cannot use the resources on the other computer. What is the best action to take?

    A. Reset the DSL modem.

    B. Replace the NIC in one computer and then the other.

    C. Delete the local connections and re-create them.

    D. Set up file sharing through Windows Explorer.

    220-702 A+ Objective 3.1, "Troubleshoot client-side connectivity issues using appropriate tools"

45. A customer has asked you to set up an SSH server. What port needs to be forwarded from the router to enable a server behind the router to accept SSH connections?

    A. 21

    B. 22

    C. 25

    D. 3389

    220-702 A+ Objective 3.2, "Install and configure a small home office (SOHO) network"

SECURITY

1. You are preparing to assign permissions to a new user on a Vista system. By default, Windows Vista offers each of these user account groups *except* which of the following?

   A. Administrator

   B. Standard user

   C. Power user

   D. Guest

   220-702 Objective 4.2, "Implement security and troubleshoot common problems"

2. You have created a folder outside of your user profile. By default, Windows gives access to that folder to whom?

   A. Everyone

   B. All authenticated users

   C. Anonymous users

   D. Only you

   220-702 Objective 4.2, "Implement security and troubleshoot common problems"

3. You are checking permissions on a Windows server you are configuring. What user group contains domain accounts, local accounts, and the Guest account, but not users logged into a local account on a remote machine that does not match an account on the machine in question?

   A. Authenticated users

   B. Everyone

   C. Anonymous users

   D. Local users

   220-702 Objective 4.2, "Implement security and troubleshoot common problems"

4. Windows XP defaults to simple file sharing. You know you should turn this off on a new client's computer. How is simple file sharing disabled?

   A. Right-click on the folder, Properties, Sharing, Simple File Sharing.

   B. Click Control Panel, Accessibility Options, Folder and File Accessibility.

   C. Click Control Panel, Folder Options, View, Advanced Settings.

   D. Right-click on the folder, Properties, Security, Advanced.

   220-702 Objective 4.2, "Implement security and troubleshoot common problems"

4

5. You are trying to set permissions for a folder, but you have a problem: you are logged on as an administrator, but the options in the Security tab are dimmed out. What is the most likely problem?

   A. Simple File Sharing is turned on.

   B. Simple File Sharing is turned off.

   C. You do not have access privileges to set permissions.

   D. Permissions are being inherited.

   220-702 Objective 4.2, "Implement security and troubleshoot common problems"

6. You are setting permissions for a folder and you need to turn off permissions inheritance. How is this done?

   A. Right-click on the folder, Properties, Sharing, Simple File Sharing.

   B. Click Control Panel, Accessibility Options, Folder and File Accessibility.

   C. Click Control Panel, Folder Options, View, Advanced Settings.

   D. Right-click on the folder, Properties, Security, Advanced.

   220-702 Objective 4.2, "Implement security and troubleshoot common problems"

7. You are setting up file sharing on a small office network. For Windows Vista to serve up shared folders, which of the following does *not* need to be turned on?

   A. Simple File Sharing

   B. File and Printer Sharing for Microsoft Networks

   C. File Sharing

   D. Public Folder Sharing

   220-702 Objective 4.2, "Implement security and troubleshoot common problems"

8. A user is having trouble accessing a shared file on a remote computer in a workgroup. To have full access to the remote computer, which of the following must be the same on both the local and remote computer?

   A. Username

   B. Password

   C. Both of the above

   D. Neither of the above

   220-702 Objective 4.2, "Implement security and troubleshoot common problems"

9. A client has asked you to set up a hidden share—a folder that is shared but does not show up in Network or My Network Places. How is this done?

   A. Right-click on the folder, Properties, Security, Advanced.

   B. Right-click on the folder, Properties, Sharing, Hidden Sharing.

   C. Add a $ symbol to the end of the folder name.

   D. Click Control Panel, Folder Options, View, Advanced Settings.

   220-702 Objective 4.2, "Implement security and troubleshoot common problems"

10. You are configuring a new computer for a client who is concerned about keeping his data secure using encryption. Which edition of Windows does *not* allow for encryption?

A. Vista Ultimate

B. Vista Business

C. XP Professional

D. Vista Home

220-702 Objective 4.2, "Implement security and troubleshoot common problems"

11. You are examining a customer's computer and see a folder's name listed in green in Windows Explorer. What does this mean?

A. The folder is shared on the network.

B. The logged-in user has access permissions to the folder.

C. The folder is encrypted.

D. None of the above.

220-702 Objective 4.2, "Implement security and troubleshoot common problems"

12. You would like to export an EFS certificate. What is the appropriate tool?

A. The Certificate Manager console.

B. The Cipher command.

C. Right-click the encrypted file, Properties, Advanced, Export Certificate.

D. This cannot be done.

220-702 Objective 4.2, "Implement security and troubleshoot common problems"

13. A customer would like to share an encrypted file with other local users of a computer system. How is this done?

A. Each local user's certificate must be added to the encrypted file.

B. Right-click on file, Properties, Security, Advanced, check Share with Local Users.

C. Right-click on file, Properties, Advanced, Encryption, check Share with Local Users.

D. This cannot be done.

220-702 Objective 4.2, "Implement security and troubleshoot common problems"

14. A customer would like to share an encrypted file with other remote users on different computers on the (nondomain) workgroup network. How is this done?

A. Each other local user's certificate must be added to the encrypted file.

B. Right-click on file, Properties, Security, Advanced, and check Share with Local Users.

C. Right-click on file, Properties, Advanced, Encryption, and check Share with Local Users.

D. This cannot be done.

220-702 Objective 4.2, "Implement security and troubleshoot common problems"

4

15. You have a client who wants his Windows system files to be encrypted. How can this be done?
    A. Using Encrypting File System (EFS) certificates
    B. Using Vista BitLocker Encryption
    C. Either of the above
    D. Neither of the above
    220-702 Objective 4.2, "Implement security and troubleshoot common problems"

16. Assuming the necessary hardware support, Vista BitLocker encryption provides what kind of authentication?
    A. Computer authentication
    B. User authentication
    C. Both of the above
    D. Neither of the above
    220-702 Objective 4.2, "Implement security and troubleshoot common problems"

17. You are servicing a computer you suspect to be infected with a virus. What should you do first?
    A. Back up any important data on the system.
    B. Use antivirus software to scan for viruses.
    C. Quarantine the system.
    D. Remediate the system.
    220-702 Objective 4.1, "Prevent, troubleshoot, and remove viruses and malware"

18. You have been asked to fix an infected computer that does not have antivirus software installed. What is the most effective way to clean the computer?
    A. Immediately download and run antivirus software from a trusted Internet site.
    B. Obtain antivirus software on CD, and use the CD to install the software on the infected computer.
    C. Connect the infected computer to an uninfected computer with antivirus software, and run the antivirus software from the uninfected computer on the C drive of the infected computer.
    D. Reformat the hard drive and reinstall Windows.
    220-702 Objective 4.1, "Prevent, troubleshoot, and remove viruses and malware"

19. When remediating an infected system, what should be done with respect to the data storage area of the System Restore utility?
    A. Use a previous restore point to restore the system to a noninfected state.
    B. Use antivirus software to clean the restore points.
    C. Turn System Protection off, reboot, and then turn System Protection back on to purge the data storage area.
    D. All of the above.
    220-702 Objective 4.1, "Prevent, troubleshoot, and remove viruses and malware"

20. While scanning the Task Manager of a system you are remediating, you see a number of svchost.exe processes. You should suspect that it is malware rather than a legitimate process if it is running under which username?

A. SYSTEM

B. LOCAL SERVICE

C. NETWORK SERVICE

D. The username of the user currently logged in

220-702 Objective 4.1, "Prevent, troubleshoot, and remove viruses and malware"

21. You are examining the Task Manager's list of running processes. Which of the following is likely not legitimate?

A. C:\Windows\system32\svchost.exe

B. C:\Program Files\Windows\system32\svchost.exe

C. C:\Program Files\MSN Messenger\Msmsgs.exe

D. C:\Windows\system32\Taskmgr.exe

220-702 Objective 4.1, "Prevent, troubleshoot, and remove viruses and malware"

22. You are examining the Task Manager's list of running processes. Which of the following is likely not legitimate?

A. C:\Windows\system32\Lsass.exe

B. System

C. C:\Windows\Explorer.exe

D. C:\Windows\Winlogon.exe

220-702 Objective 4.1, "Prevent, troubleshoot, and remove viruses and malware"

23. You are administering a computer with local shares for several users with similar job needs. What is the easiest way to give everyone the appropriate access?

A. Assign permissions to each user.

B. Assign permissions to user groups, and place the appropriate users in the appropriate groups.

C. Make a copy of the appropriate shared data for each user with similar needs.

D. Allow global access to all users.

220-702 Objective 4.2, "Implement security and troubleshoot common problems"

24. You are setting permissions for a file in a folder that has permissions propagated from its parent folder. What effect will the explicit permissions have?

A. They will override the inherited permissions.

B. None—they will be overridden by the inherited permissions.

C. They will be combined with the inherited permissions in the least restrictive way.

D. They will be combined with the inherited permissions in the most restrictive way.

220-702 Objective 4.2, "Implement security and troubleshoot common problems"

4

25. You are configuring a network-accessible folder. What kind of permissions apply to remote users of a file or folder?

A. Regular permissions

B. Share permissions

C. Administrative permissions

D. All of the above

220-702 Objective 4.2, "Implement security and troubleshoot common problems"

26. For the administrative share *computername**admin$* to be automatically enabled and accessible to administrators, what condition must hold?

A. The computer must be in a workgroup.

B. The computer must be in a domain.

C. The computer must have administrative shares enabled.

D. The folder C:\Users\Public\admin$ must be created on the computer *computername*.

220-702 Objective 4.2, "Implement security and troubleshoot common problems"

27. As an administrator on a domain, you would like to be able to easily access any drive or volume on any computer on the domain. How can this be done?

A. This cannot be done because it isn't allowed.

B. You must manually set up the network shares and permissions appropriately for each volume on each computer.

C. Enter the computer name and then the drive name followed by a $ (for example, *computername**C$*) in the Explorer address bar.

D. Navigate to the desired drive using My Network Places.

220-702 Objective 4.2, "Implement security and troubleshoot common problems"

28. You are configuring a computer that will be used with Vista BitLocker. What hardware support is needed to support Vista BitLocker computer authentication?

A. A S.M.A.R.T.-compatible hard drive

B. A TPM chip on the motherboard

C. A USB flash drive with the authentication key

D. None of the above

220-702 Objective 4.2, "Implement security and troubleshoot common problems"

29. You are setting permissions for a client's data, which is held in a folder with 30 subfolders and files. What is the easiest way to set the permissions for all 30 subfolders and files?

A. Set the permissions for each folder or file individually.

B. Change the ownership of each file or folder.

C. Move the data to an encrypted volume.

D. Use inherited permissions propagated from the parent folder.

220-702 Objective 4.2, "Implement security and troubleshoot common problems"

30. You want to make a backup of an EFS certificate. What command should you enter in the Vista Start Search box or the XP Run box?

    A. efsbkup.cmd

    B. certmgr.msc

    C. certexp.exe

    D. certbkup.msc

    220-702 Objective 4.2, "Implement security and troubleshoot common problems"

31. You are exporting a certificate file so that another user can add it to let you read an encrypted file. You load the .pfx file on a USB flash drive and prepare to bring the drive to the computer with the encrypted file. What is the potential danger here?

    A. No significant danger—this is the appropriate procedure for gaining access to an encrypted file.

    B. If you lose the USB flash drive, you will not be able to recover your data.

    C. The .pfx file also contains your private key, which you should not share.

    D. The flash drive may contain a virus.

    220-702 Objective 4.2, "Implement security and troubleshoot common problems"

32. A client has asked you to encrypt a folder on her computer for security. You follow the correct procedure but discover that the check box Encrypt Contents to Secure Data is dimmed. What is the most likely problem?

    A. The folder is already encrypted.

    B. The volume is not using NTFS.

    C. Some kind of malware is interfering with encryption functionality.

    D. The version of Windows you are using does not support encryption.

    220-702 Objective 4.2, "Implement security and troubleshoot common problems"

33. A client has asked you to encrypt a folder on her computer for security. You follow the correct procedure but discover that the Advanced button is missing on the General tab of the folder's properties box. What is the most likely problem?

    A. The folder is already encrypted.

    B. The volume is not using the NTFS.

    C. Some kind of malware is interfering with encryption functionality.

    D. The version of Windows you are using does not support encryption.

    220-702 Objective 4.2, "Implement security and troubleshoot common problems"

34. Pop-up ads plague you when surfing the Web, your system generally works much slower than it used to, and disk access seems excessive even for simple tasks. What do these symptoms suggest?

    A. The system is infected with malware.

    B. Windows Software Update needs to be run.

    C. You are using a system with Vista BitLocker on the system files.

    D. The hard drive is failing.

    220-702 Objective 4.1, "Prevent, troubleshoot, and remove viruses and malware"

4

35. Your client would like to use BitLocker with his system. What is the major danger of using BitLocker computer authentication with important data?

    A. If the hard drive is stolen from the computer, the data can be accessed by installing the hard drive in another computer.

    B. If the motherboard fails and is replaced, the data cannot be accessed without a backup copy of the startup key.

    C. A careless user will leave a USB flash drive with the startup key near the computer.

    D. There are only 256 possible startup keys, so with a little time, an intruder can gain access to the data.

    220-702 Objective 4.2, "Implement security and troubleshoot common problems"

36. You are removing a hard drive from a client's computer and installing it on a different computer. Will a BIOS drive lock password-protect the data from unauthorized access?

    A. No, because the new computer may have a different BIOS.

    B. No, that is the specific contingency a drive lock password is intended to guard against.

    C. Yes.

    D. It depends on the system.

    220-702 Objective 4.2, "Implement security and troubleshoot common problems"

37. Your client often works on encrypted files. For additional security, which of the following should be disabled while working on an encrypted file?

    A. Antivirus software

    B. Hibernation

    C. Automatic Windows Software Update

    D. BitLocker Encryption

    220-702 Objective 4.2, "Implement security and troubleshoot common problems"

38. If the BIOS supervisor password is set and forgotten, BIOS setup cannot be entered. How can you get around this problem?

    A. Hold down the Ctrl, Alt, Shift, and B keys while booting to reset the BIOS.

    B. Use motherboard jumpers to reset the BIOS.

    C. Mount the hard drive using another computer and use the Cipher program to retrieve the password.

    D. Any of the above will work.

    220-702 Objective 4.2, "Implement security and troubleshoot common problems"

39. You are having trouble installing BitLocker and want to try clearing the TPM chip. How is this done?

    A. Enter tpmreset.exe in the Vista Start Search box.

    B. Enter tpm.msc in the Vista Start Search box.

    C. Hold down the Ctrl, Shift, Alt, and T keys while booting.

    D. This can only be done by the motherboard manufacturer.

    220-702 Objective 4.2, "Implement security and troubleshoot common problems"

Part III

CompTIA A+
Exam Answers

CompTIA A+ 220-701 Essentials Exam Answers

CompTIA A+ 220-702 Practical Applications Exam Answers

COMPTIA A+ 220-701
ESSENTIALS EXAM ANSWERS

DOMAIN 1.0 HARDWARE

Question	Answer	Explanation
1	B	ATX (Advanced Technology Extended) is the most commonly used form factor today.
2	D	The first ATX power supplies and motherboards used a single power connector called the P1 connector.
3	A	If an operating system supports the soft switch, it can turn off the power to a system after the shutdown procedure is complete.
4	B	The MicroATX form factor is a major variation of ATX that addresses some technologies that have emerged since the original development of ATX.
5	B	MicroATX reduces the total cost of a system by reducing the number of expansion slots on the motherboard, reducing the power supplied to the board, and allowing a smaller case size.
6	C	FlexATX is commonly used in slimline and all-in-one cases but can fit into any FlexATX, MicroATX, or ATX case that follows the ATX 2.03 or higher standard.
7	A	The BTX (Balanced Technology Extended) form factor was designed by Intel in 2003 for flexibility and can be used by everything from large tower systems to those ultrasmall systems that sit under a monitor.
8	A	The BTX form factor design focuses on reducing heat with better airflow and improved fans and coolers.
9	D	The NLX (New Low-profile Extended) form factor for low-end personal computer motherboards was developed by Intel in 1998 to improve on an older and similar form factor, called the LPX form factor.
10	B	The riser card on an NLX motherboard is on the edge of the board.

A

Question	Answer	Explanation
11	D	The computer case, sometimes called the chassis, houses the power supply, motherboard, expansion cards, and drives.
12	C	The first LGA socket is the LGA775 socket.
13	A	The X58 chipset supports the Intel LGA1366 socket, the Core i7 processors, and PCI Express Version 2.
14	D	A bus that does not run in sync with the system clock is called an expansion bus and always connects to the slow end of the chipset, the South Bridge.
15	B	The first PCI bus had a 32-bit data path, supplied 5 V of power to an expansion card, and operated at 33 MHz.
16	C	Throughput is sometimes called bandwidth.
17	A	PCI-X is focused on technologies that target the server market.
18	C	A PCI Express x1 slot contains a single lane for data, which is actually four wires.
19	C	PCIe Version 2 doubled the frequency of the PCIe bus, theoretically doubling the throughput.
20	D	You can use a riser card in other systems besides NLX to extend an expansion slot.
21	B	APG 3.0 cards can be installed in an AGP 1.5-V slot, but signals are put on the data bus using 0.8 V.
22	C	Part of a riser card's audio, modem, or networking logic is on the card, and part is on a controller on the motherboard.
23	C	A CNR slot is smaller than a PCI slot but about the same height.
24	D	Ports coming directly off the motherboard are called on-board ports or integrated components.
25	B	A motherboard might have several internal connectors, including parallel ATA connectors (also called EIDE connectors), a floppy drive connector, serial ATA connectors, SCSI connectors, or a FireWire (IEEE 1394) connector.
26	A	A program in BIOS, called BIOS setup or CMOS setup, can easily make changes to the setup values stored in CMOS RAM.
27	C	Some older motherboards and expansion cards store setup data using a dual inline package (DIP) switch.
28	D	You do not have to replace an entire motherboard if one port fails.
29	C	Jumpers are considered open or closed based on whether a jumper cover is present on two small posts or metal pins that stick up off the motherboard.

Question	Answer	Explanation
30	B	Setup information about the motherboard can be stored by setting a jumper on (closed) or off (open).
31	A	The term *booting* comes from the phrase "lifting yourself up by your bootstraps" and refers to the computer bringing itself up to a working state without the user having to do anything but press the on button.
32	A	A hard boot, or cold boot, involves turning on the power with the on/off switch.
33	C	A soft boot, or warm boot, involves using the operating system to reboot.
34	B	The startup BIOS is programming contained on the firmware chip on the motherboard that is responsible for getting a system up and going and finding an OS to load.
35	B	The startup BIOS surveys hardware resources and needs and assigns system resources to meet those needs.
36	B	The startup BIOS begins the startup process by reading configuration information stored primarily in CMOS RAM and then comparing that information to the hardware: the processor, video slot, PCI slots, hard drive, and so on.
37	D	At the beginning of the boot drive (usually drive C) is the OS boot record.
38	D	This OS boot record contains a small program that points to a larger OS program file that is responsible for starting the OS load.
39	B	A program file contains a list of instructions stored in a file.
40	A	For Windows Vista, the OS boot record program points to BootMgr.
41	C	For Windows XP, Ntldr is responsible for loading the OS, and is, therefore, called the boot loader program.
42	D	EFI (Extensible Firmware Interface) and UEFI (Unified EFI) are two standards for the interface between firmware on the motherboard and the operating system.
43	B	The GPT (Globally Unique Identifier Partition Table) disk partitioning system can support up to 128 partitions.
44	C	A processor contains three basic components: an input/output (I/O) unit, a control unit, and one or more arithmetic logic units (ALUs).
45	A	Registers hold counters, data, instructions, and addresses that the ALU is currently processing.
46	D	The portion of the internal bus that connects the processor to the internal memory cache is called the back-side bus (BSB).
47	B	Processor frequency is the speed at which the processor operates internally.

A

Question	Answer	Explanation
48	C	Running a motherboard or processor at a higher speed than the manufacturer suggests is called overclocking.
49	A	The cooler sits on top of the processor and consists of a fan and a heat sink.
50	B	A peltier is a heat sink carrying an electrical charge that causes it to act as an electrical thermal transfer device.
51	A	The most popular method of cooling overclocked processors is a liquid cooling system.
52	C	Instead of processing data for each beat of the system clock, as regular SDRAM does, DDR processes data when the beat rises and again when it falls, doubling the data rate of memory.
53	B	A hard disk drive (HDD), most often called a hard drive, comes in two sizes for personal computers: the 2.5-inch size used for laptop computers and the 3.5-inch size used for desktops.
54	C	A magnetic hard drive has one, two, or more platters, or disks, that stack together and spin in unison inside a sealed metal housing that contains firmware to control reading and writing data to the drive and to communicate with the motherboard.
55	D	All the read/write heads are controlled by an actuator, which moves the read/write heads across the disk surfaces in unison.
56	A	Each side, or surface, of one hard drive platter is called a head.
57	B	The ATA interface standards define how hard drives and other drives such as CD, DVD, tape, and Blu-ray drives interface with a computer system.
58	C	S.M.A.R.T. (Self-Monitoring Analysis and Reporting Technology) is a system BIOS feature that monitors hard drive performance, disk spin up time, temperature, distance between the head and the disk, and other mechanical activities of the drive to predict when the drive is likely to fail.
59	B	Parallel ATA, also called the EIDE (Enhanced IDE) standard or, more loosely, the IDE (Integrated Drive Electronics) standard, allows for one or two IDE connectors on a motherboard, each using a 40-pin data cable.
60	A	The 80-conductor IDE cable has 40 pins and 80 wires.
61	D	DMA transfers data directly from the drive to memory without involving the CPU.
62	B	Serial ATA interfaces are much faster than PATA interfaces and are used by all types of drives, including hard drives, CD, DVD, Blu-ray, and tape drives.
63	C	External SATA (eSATA) is up to six times faster than USB or FireWire.

Question	Answer	Explanation
64	C	If a motherboard does not have an embedded SCSI controller, the gateway from the SCSI bus to the system bus is the SCSI host adapter card, commonly called the host adapter.
65	C	A host adapter can support both internal and external SCSI devices, using one connector on the card for a ribbon cable or round cable to connect to internal devices, and an external port that supports external devices.
66	B	Each device on the bus is assigned a number from 0 to 15 called the SCSI ID, by means of DIP switches, dials on the device, or software settings.
67	A	To reduce the amount of electrical "noise," or interference, on a SCSI cable, each end of the SCSI chain has a terminating resistor.
68	B	A technology that configures two or more hard drives to work together as an array of drives is called RAID (redundant array of inexpensive disks or redundant array of independent disks).
69	D	Fault tolerance is a computer's ability to respond to a fault or catastrophe, such as a hardware failure or power outage.
70	A	RAID 0 uses space from two or more physical disks to increase the disk space available for a single volume.
71	A	Windows calls RAID 0 a striped volume.
72	B	RAID 1 is a type of drive imaging. It duplicates data on one drive to another drive and is used for fault tolerance.
73	C	A drive image is a duplication of everything written to a hard drive.
74	B	Windows calls RAID 1 a mirrored volume.
75	C	RAID 5 stripes data across three or more drives and uses parity checking so that if one drive fails, the other drives can re-create the data stored on the failed drive.
76	D	The boot sector, or boot record, contains the information about how the disk is organized and which file system is used.
77	C	A 3 1/2-inch high-density floppy disk has 224 entries in the root directory.
78	B	As many as 127 USB devices can be daisy chained together using USB cables.
79	C	FireWire and i.Link are common names for another peripheral bus officially named IEEE 1394 (or sometimes simply called 1394).
80	D	IEEE 1394a supports two types of connectors and cables: a 4-pin connector that does not provide voltage to a device and a 6-pin connector that does.

A

Question	Answer	Explanation
81	A	IEEE 1394 uses isochronous data transfer, meaning that data is transferred continuously without breaks.
82	D	Because DIMMs use a 64-bit data path, it takes only a single DIMM to provide one memory bank to the processor.
83	C	The controller logic on a motherboard that manages serial ports is called UART (Universal Asynchronous Receiver-Transmitter) or UART 16550.
84	A	The standard parallel port is sometimes called a normal parallel port or a Centronics port.
85	C	An infrared transceiver, also called an IrDA (Infrared Data Association) transceiver or an IR transceiver, provides an infrared port for wireless communication.
86	B	The primary output device of a computer is the monitor.
87	D	A pixel is formed by the intersection of the row and column electrodes.
88	D	The refresh rate is the number of times one screen or frame is built in one second.
89	C	The screen size is the diagonal length of the screen's surface.
90	A	Native resolution is the number of pixels built into the LCD monitor.
91	B	Interlaced CRT monitors draw a screen by making two passes.
92	D	A noninterlaced monitor (also called a progressive monitor) draws the entire screen in one pass.
93	A	For CRT monitors, resolution is a measure of how many pixels on a CRT screen are addressable by software.
94	C	Whereas a CRT monitor is designed to use several resolutions, an LCD monitor uses only one resolution, called the native resolution.
95	D	VGA (Video Graphics Array) supports up to 640 |ts| 480, which is a 4:3 ratio between horizontal pixels and vertical pixels.
96	C	SVGA (Super VGA) supports up to 800 |ts| 600 resolution.
97	A	SXGA (Super XGA) supports up to 1280 |ts| 1024 resolution and was the first to use a 5:4 ratio between horizontal pixels and vertical pixels.
98	B	QWXGA (Quad Wide XGA) supports up to 2048 |ts| 1152 and is used by 23-inch monitors.
99	B	A 15-pin VGA port is the standard analog video method of passing three separate signals for red, green, and blue (RGB), which older video cards and CRT monitors use.
100	C	DVI (Digital Visual Interface) is the digital interface standard used by digital monitors, such as a digital LCD monitor and digital TVs (HDTV).

Question	Answer	Explanation
101	A	Using the composite port, the red, green, and blue (RGB) are mixed together in the same signal.
102	D	An S-Video port sends two signals over the cable—one for color and the other for brightness—and is used by some high-end TVs and video equipment.
103	C	The more RAM installed on the card, the better the performance.
104	D	A fan card installs in a slot and provides one or two fans used to cool cards in adjacent slots.
105	A	TIFF (tagged image file format) files are larger than JPEG files, but retain more image information and give better results when printing photographs.
106	C	MIDI (musical instrument digital interface), pronounced "middy," is a set of standards used to represent music in digital form.
107	B	A port replicator provides ports to allow a notebook to easily connect to a full-sized monitor, keyboard, AC power adapter, and other peripheral devices.
108	D	A docking station provides the same functions as a port replicator but also provides additional slots for adding secondary storage devices and expansion cards.
109	A	PCMIA cards are used by many devices, including modems, network cards for wired or wireless networks, sound cards, SCSI host adapters, IEEE 1394 controllers, USB controllers, flash memory adapters, TV tuners, and hard disks.
110	C	CardBus slots improved PC Card slots by increasing the bus width to 32 bits, while maintaining backward compatibility with earlier standards.
111	B	You can install an Internet card to connect to a cellular mobile phone network.
112	D	A DMFC initially provides up to 5 hours of battery life, and future versions will provide up to 10 hours of battery life.
113	A	An inverter is an electrical device that changes DC to AC.
114	C	The most common pointing device on a notebook is a touch pad.
115	C	A laser printer is a type of electrophotographic printer that can range from a small, personal desktop model to a large, network printer capable of handling and printing large volumes continuously.
116	A	A laser printer can produce better-quality printouts than a dot matrix printer, even when printing at the same dpi, because it can vary the size of the dots it prints, creating a sharp, clear image. Hewlett-Packard (HP) calls this technology of varying the size of dots REt (Resolution Enhancement technology).

A

Question	Answer	Explanation
117	B	Inkjet printers use a type of ink-dispersion printing and don't normally provide the high-quality resolution of laser printers, but they are popular because they are small and can print color inexpensively.
118	C	An impact printer creates a printed page by using some mechanism that touches or hits the paper.
119	C	Thermal printers use wax-based ink that is heated by heat pins that melt the ink onto paper.
120	A	A dye-sublimation printer uses solid dyes embedded on different transparent films.
121	B	Solid ink printers use ink stored in solid blocks, which Xerox calls color sticks.
122	C	A local printer connects directly to a computer by way of a USB port, parallel port, serial port, wireless connection (Bluetooth, infrared, or Wi-Fi), IEEE 1394 (FireWire) port, SCSI port, PC Card, or ExpressCard connection.
123	B	A network printer has an Ethernet port to connect directly to the network.
124	A	A network printer is identified on the network by its IP address.
125	D	Group Policy under Windows Vista can be used to limit and control all kinds of printer-related tasks, including the number of printers that can be installed using the Add Printer Wizard, how print jobs are sent to print servers (rendered or not rendered), which print servers the computer can use, and which printers on a network the computer can use.
126	B	When working with laser printer toner cartridges, if you get toner dust on your clothes or hands while exchanging the cartridge, don't use hot water to clean it up.
127	A	Laser printers require the interaction of mechanical, electrical, and optical technologies to work.
128	C	A sweeper strip cleans the drum of any residual toner, which is swept away by a sweeping blade.
129	D	A laser beam discharges a lower charge only to places where toner should go.
130	A	A control blade prevents too much toner from sticking to the cylinder surface.
131	D	Photos printed on an inkjet printer tend to fade over time, more so than photos produced professionally.
132	A	A thermal printer can burn dots onto special paper, as done by older fax machines (called direct thermal printing), or the printer can use a ribbon that contains the wax-based ink (called thermal wax transfer printing).

Question	Answer	Explanation
133	B	To know the IP address of a network printer, direct the printer to print a configuration page, which should include its IP address.
134	B	Memory in the processor package, but not on the processor die, is called Level 2 cache (L2 cache).
135	D	Multiprocessing is the ability of a system to do more than one thing at a time.

DOMAIN 2.0 TROUBLESHOOTING, REPAIR, AND MAINTENANCE

Question	Answer	Explanation
1	C	In BIOS setup, disable the ability to write to the boot sector of the hard drive. This alone can keep boot viruses at bay.
2	C	Chips and expansion cards should be firmly seated.
3	C	To maintain the hard drive, rearrange noncontiguous parts of files (called defragmenting the drive), delete unnecessary files, and check the drive for errors.
4	B	To clean up the start routine, delete temporary files and check the hard drive for errors.
5	A	To maintain your computer's security, verify that Windows has all updates and patches installed and that Windows is set to automatically download and install updates.
6	D	Windows needs free space on the hard drive for normal operation, for defragmenting the drive, for burning CDs and DVDs, and for a variety of other tasks.
7	B	Fragmentation may cause the hard drive to slow down.
8	B	Defragmenting rearranges files on the drive into as few segments as possible.
9	A	To fully defragment the drive, 15 percent of the drive must be free.
10	C	To make sure the drive is healthy, you need to search for and repair file system errors using the Windows Chkdsk utility.
11	C	The *chkdsk* utility searches for bad sectors on a volume and recovers the data from them if possible.
12	D	The Windows 9x/Me command, Scandisk C, is equivalent to Chkdsk C: /R in Windows Vista/XP/2000.
13	C	A backup is an extra copy of a data or software file that you can use if the original file becomes damaged or destroyed.

A

Question	Answer	Explanation
14	A	Windows XP/2000 offers the Ntbackup.exe program to back up files and folders.
15	D	Backups of important and sensitive data should be kept under lock and key.
16	C	With a full backup, all files selected for backup are copied to the backup media. Each file is marked as backed up by clearing its archive attribute.
17	A	With a copy backup, all files selected for backup are copied to the backup media, but files are not marked as backed up (meaning file archive attributes are not cleared).
18	B	With an incremental backup, all files that have been created or changed since the last backup are backed up, and all files are marked as backed up (meaning file archive attributes are cleared).
19	D	With a differential backup, all files that have been created or changed since the last full or incremental backup are backed up, and files are not marked as backed up.
20	A	With a daily backup, all files that have been created or changed on this day are backed up. Files are not marked as backed up.
21	B	Windows Vista and XP use System Restore to keep backups of critical system files.
22	D	System state data is made up of files critical to a successful operating system load.
23	C	System Restore restores the system to its condition at the time a snapshot was taken of the system settings and configuration.
24	A	System Protection creates restore points at regular intervals and just before you install software or hardware.
25	B	The restore process cannot remove a virus or worm infection.
26	D	A Complete PC backup makes a backup of the entire volume on which Vista is installed and can also back up other volumes.
27	C	Complete PC backup is not available in Vista Starter or Vista Home editions.
28	B	You can quickly identify a problem with memory or eliminate memory as the source of a problem by using the Vista Memory Diagnostics tool.
29	A	System File Checker (SFC) is a Windows Vista and XP utility that protects system files and keeps a cache of current system files in case it needs to refresh a damaged file.
30	D	Driver Verifier (verifier.exe) is a Windows Vista/XP/2000 utility that runs in the background to put stress on drivers as they are loaded and running.

Question	Answer	Explanation
31	C	The File Signature Verification tool displays information about digitally signed files, including device driver files and application files, and logs information to C:\Windows\Sigverif.txt.
32	B	The Driver Query tool can be used to direct information about drivers to a file, including information about digital signatures.
33	D	A system lockup means that the computer freezes and must be restarted.
34	A	The *bootrec /scanOS* command scans the hard drive for Windows installations not stored in the BCD.
35	D	The *bootrec /fixboot* command repairs the boot sector of the system partition.
36	B	The *diskpart* command manages partitions and volume.
37	C	*Ntldr* is a boot-strap loader program.
38	D	The *boot.ini* file text file contains boot parameters.
39	B	The *bootsect.dos* file is used to load another OS in a dual-boot environment.
40	A	*Ntdetect* is a real-mode program that detects hardware.
41	C	The *ntbootdd.sys* file is required only if a SCSI boot device is used.
42	B	*Ntoskrnl.exe* is a core component of the OS executive and kernel services.
43	D	*Pagefile.sys* is a virtual memory swap file.
44	A	There are two main sections in Boot.ini: the [boot loader] section and the [operating systems] section.
45	C	Use the Recovery Console when Windows 2000/XP does not start properly or hangs during the load. It works even when core Windows system files are corrupted.
46	B	The Recovery Console allows you to enable or disable a service or device driver.
47	B	The Recovery Console is designed so that someone cannot maliciously use it to gain unauthorized access.
48	A	The *cd* command displays or changes the current folder.
49	D	The *dir* command is used to list files and folders.
50	B	The *diskpart* command creates and deletes partitions on the hard drive.
51	A	The *fixmbr* command rewrites the Master Boot Record boot program.
52	D	The *listsvc* command lists all available services.
53	C	The *map* command lists all drive letters and file system types.

A

Question	Answer	Explanation
54	B	The *systemroot* command sets the current directory to the directory where Windows 2000/XP is installed.
55	C	The *set* command displays or sets Recovery Console environmental variables.
56	D	The *Fixmbr* command restores the master boot program in the MBR.
57	B	The *Fixboot* command repairs the OS boot record.
58	A	Use the *Diskpart* command to view, create, and delete partitions on the drive.
59	C	The *chkdsk* command repairs the file system and recovers data from bad sectors.
60	D	The *map* command is useful to find your way around the system, such as when you need to know the drive letter for the CD drive.
61	A	The *bootcfg* command allows you to view and edit the Boot.ini file.
62	C	The Windows 2000 Emergency Repair Process should be used only as a last resort because it restores the system to the state it was in immediately after the Windows 2000 installation.
63	A	Notebooks use the same technology as PCs, but with modifications to use less power, take up less space, and operate on the move.
64	B	Warranties can be voided by opening the case, removing part labels, installing other-vendor parts, upgrading the OS, or disassembling the system unless directly instructed to do so by the service center help desk personnel.
65	D	An example of diagnostic software is PC-Doctor.
66	B	You should not pick up or hold the notebook by the display panel.
67	D	The touch pad is the most common pointing device on a notebook.
68	A	IBM and Lenovo ThinkPad notebooks use a unique and popular pointing device embedded in the keyboard called a TrackPoint or point stick.
69	C	An input device that can be used to hand draw is the graphics tablet.
70	C	Graphics tablets are popular with graphics artists and others who use desktop publishing applications.
71	A	Ntbackup.exe is used to restore the system state, data, and software from previously made backups.
72	C	Boot logging uses events logged to the Ntbtlog.txt file to investigate the source of an unknown startup error.
73	D	Cacls.exe is used to gain access to a file when permissions to the file are in error or corrupted.

Question	Answer	Explanation
74	B	Cipher.exe is used to decrypt a file that is not available because the user account that encrypted the file is no longer accessible.
75	A	The Compact.exe tool can be used with an NTFS file system to display and change the compressions applied to files and folders.
76	D	The Computer Management tool can be used to access several snap-ins to manage and troubleshoot a system.
77	B	The Device Driver Roll Back tool can be used to replace a driver with the one that worked before the current driver was installed.
78	A	The Disk Cleanup tool can be used to delete unused files to make more disk space available.
79	C	The Disk Management tool can be used to view and change partitions on hard drives and to format drives.
80	A	The Driver Verifier tool can be used to identify a driver that is causing a problem.
81	B	Group Policy can be used to display and change policies controlling users and the computer.
82	D	Last Known Good Configuration can be used when Windows won't start normally and you want to revert the system to before a Windows setting, driver, or application that is causing problems was changed.
83	B	Performance Monitor can be used to view information about performance to help you identify a performance bottleneck.
84	C	The Program Compatibility Wizard can be used to resolve issues that prevent legacy software from working.
85	A	The Programs and Features window can be used to uninstall, repair, or update software or certain device drivers that are causing a problem.
86	D	The Recovery Console can be used to troubleshoot a Windows XP/2000 startup problem and recover data from the hard drive.
87	C	Runas.exe allows you to run a program using different permissions from those assigned to the currently logged-on user.
88	B	SC can be used to stop or start a service that runs in the background.
89	D	Software Explorer can be used to view and change programs launched at startup.
90	C	Msconfig.exe troubleshoots the startup process by temporarily disabling startup programs and services.
91	A	System File Checker is useful when you suspect system files are corrupted, but you can still access the Windows desktop.

A

Question	Answer	Explanation
92	D	System Information is used to display information about hardware, applications, and Windows.
93	C	The Task Killing Utility is useful when managing background services such as an e-mail server or Web server.
94	D	Task Manager is useful when you need to stop a locked-up application.
95	B	Windows Defender monitors activity and alerts you if a running program appears to be malicious or damaging the system.
96	D	Windows File Protection runs in the background to protect system files and restore overwritten system files as needed.
97	A	Windows Firewall runs in the background to prevent or filter uninvited communication from another computer.
98	B	PostScript is a language used to communicate how a page is to print and was developed by Adobe Systems.
99	D	Printer Control Language was developed by Hewlett-Packard but is considered a de facto standard in the printing industry.
100	A	Text data that contains no embedded control characters is sent to the printer as is, and the printer can print it without processing. The data is called raw data.

DOMAIN 3.0 OPERATING SYSTEMS AND SOFTWARE

Question	Answer	Explanation
1	D	The operating system manages hardware, runs applications, provides an interface for users, and stores, retrieves, and manipulates files.
2	B	Windows XP is an upgrade of Windows 2000 and attempts to integrate Windows 9x/Me and 2000.
3	C	Windows XP is the first Windows OS to allow multiple users to log on simultaneously to the OS.
4	A	A service pack is a major update or fix to an OS occasionally released by Microsoft.
5	D	Minor updates or fixes that are released more frequently are called patches.
6	A	Vista has a new 3D user interface called the Aero user interface.
7	B	A thread is a single task, such as the task of printing a file that the process requests from the kernel.
8	A	32-bit processors are known as x86 processors because Intel used the number 86 in the model number of these earlier processors.

Question	Answer	Explanation
9	D	Windows 2000 is a 32-bit OS.
10	B	A 64-bit OS requires more resources than a 32-bit OS.
11	C	The term x86-64 refers to a 64-bit OS or to 32-bit processors that process 64-bit instructions such as the Intel Core2 Duo or 64-bit AMD processor.
12	A	The term IA64 refers specifically to 64-bit Intel processors such as the Xeon or Itanium.
13	D	System Restore is *not* an available option for launching an application.
14	C	The taskbar is normally located at the bottom of the Windows desktop, displaying information about open programs and providing quick access to others.
15	B	The notification area is usually on the right side of the taskbar and displays open services.
16	D	A service is a program that runs in the background to support or serve Windows or an application.
17	C	The term *file extension* refers to one or more characters following the last period in a filename, such as .exe, .txt, or .avi.
18	C	The file extension indicates how the file is organized or formatted, the type content in the file, and what program uses the file.
19	D	A new security feature introduced with Windows Vista is the User Account Control (UAC) dialog box.
20	A	In Vista, there are two types of user accounts: administrator account and standard account.
21	C	The purpose of the UAC box is to prevent malicious background tasks from doing harm when the administrator is logged on.
22	A	If the top of the UAC box is red, Vista does not trust this program and is not happy with your installing it.
23	D	If the top of the UAC box is yellow, Vista does not know or trust the publisher.
24	C	If the top of the UAC box is green, Vista is happy to accept one of its own Windows components to be installed.
25	B	If the top of the UAC box is gray, the program has signed in with Microsoft, and Vista is happy to install it.
26	B	Every OS manages a hard drive, optical drive, floppy disk, or USB drive by using directories (also called folders), subdirectories, and files.
27	A	When you refer to a drive and directories that are pointing to the location of a file, as in C:\Data\Business\Letter.docx, the drive and directories are called the path.

A

Question	Answer	Explanation
28	C	The .docx file extension identifies a file type as a Microsoft Word 2007 document file.
29	A	In Windows 2000/XP, the user folder is also named after the user account name. The folder is created under the %SystemDrive%\Documents and Settings folder.
30	C	Using Explorer or the Computer window, you can view and change the properties assigned to a file; these properties are called the file attributes.
31	A	An index is a list of items that is used to speed up a search, and Vista is the first Windows OS to use indexing for its searches.
32	B	The Control Panel is a window containing several small utility programs called applets that are used to manage hardware, software, users, and the system.
33	D	The System Information Utility gives a wealth of information about installed hardware and software, the current system configuration, and currently running programs.
34	A	Windows Vista has two levels of Command Prompt windows: a standard window and an elevated window.
35	D	Windows Vista Starter has the most limited features and is intended to be used in developing nations.
36	C	Windows Vista Home Basic is similar to Windows XP Home Edition and is designed for low-cost home systems that do not require full security and networking features.
37	B	Windows Vista Home Premium is similar to Windows Vista Home Basic but includes additional features such as the Aero user interface.
38	D	Windows Vista Ultimate includes every Windows Vista feature.
39	B	Windows XP Media Center Edition is an enhanced edition of Windows XP Professional and includes additional support for digital entertainment hardware such as video recording integrated with TV input.
40	D	Dual boot allows you to install the new OS without disturbing the old one so you can boot to either OS.
41	B	An unattended installation is performed by storing the answers to installation questions in a text file or script that Windows calls an answer file.
42	C	Drive imaging is a copy of the entire volume on which Windows is installed to another bootable medium such as a CD or USB drive.
43	A	Images are created to make it easier to recover a hard drive from a catastrophic failure or to make it easier to deploy Windows and applications to many computers in a corporation.

Question	Answer	Explanation
44	D	The original drive image is created by first installing Windows and then using sysprep.exe to remove configuration settings, such as the computer name that uniquely identifies the PC.
45	B	The term virtual computer refers to software that simulates the hardware of a physical computer.
46	A	The two most popular virtual machine programs for Windows are Virtual PC by Microsoft and VMWare, Inc.
47	B	The advantages of an upgrade installation are that all applications and data and most OS settings are carried forward into the new Windows environment, and the installation is faster.
48	D	MBR keeps track of where the partitions are located on the drive, the size of each partition, and which partition is the active partition (the bootable partition).
49	A	The active partition is always the primary partition.
50	C	The system partition is the active partition of the hard drive.
51	A	The boot partition is the partition where the Windows operating system is stored.
52	B	One reason to use more than one volume on the drive is if you plan to install more than one OS on the hard drive, creating a dual-boot system.
53	A	NTFS uses smaller cluster sizes than FAT32, which means it makes more efficient use of disk space when storing many small files.
54	A	NTFS supports encryption and disk quotas (limiting the hard drive space available to a user).
55	C	FAT32 supports compression of an entire volume but not compression of individual files or folders.
56	B	Windows workgroup is a logical group of computers and users that share resources where administration, resources, and security on a workstation are controlled by that workstation.
57	C	A peer-to-peer network is one that is managed by each computer without centralized control.
58	D	A Windows domain is a group of networked computers that share a centralized directory database of user account information and security for the entire group of computers.
59	A	A client/server network is one in which the resources are managed by a centralized computer.
60	D	Windows Server 2008 controls a network using the directory database called Active Directory.

A

Question	Answer	Explanation
61	B	The User State Migration Tool is a command-line tool that works only when the new Windows Vista or XP system is a member of a Windows domain.
62	A	The scanstate command is used to copy the information from the old computer to a server or removable media.
63	D	The loadstate command is used to copy the information to the new computer.
64	B	After you have installed Vista, you need to verify that you have network access.
65	S	Product activation is a method used by Microsoft to prevent unlicensed use of its software so that you must purchase a Windows license for each installation of Windows.
66	C	Winnt.exe can be used for a clean install on a computer running MS-DOS, but not to perform an upgrade.
67	D	Setup lists all partitions that it finds on the hard drive, the file system of each partition, and the size of the partition.
68	B	Task Manager lets you view the applications and processes running on your computer as well as information about process and memory performance, network activity, and user activity.
69	C	The Processes tab lists system services and other processes associated with applications, together with how much CPU time and memory the process uses.
70	B	The Services tab lists the services currently installed along with the status.
71	D	The Performance tab provides details about how a program uses system resources.
72	D	On the Performance tab of Task Manager, the CPU Usage graph indicates the percentage of time the CPU is currently being used.
73	A	On the Performance tab of Task Manager, the Physical Memory Usage History graph shows how much memory has recently been used.
74	B	On the Performance tab of Task Manager, the Kernel Memory frame indicates how much RAM and virtual memory the core kernel components of Windows are using.
75	C	On the Performance tab of Task Manager, the System frame lists Handles (number of running objects used by all processes), Threads (number of sub-processes), Processes (number of running processes), Up Time (time since the computer was last restarted), and Page File (the first number is the amount of RAM and virtual memory currently in use, and the second number is the total RAM and virtual memory).

Question	Answer	Explanation
76	B	The Task Manager can be used to find out what processes are launched at startup and to temporarily disable a process from loading.
77	A	The Services console is used to control the Windows and third-party services installed on a system.
78	C	Computer Management is a window that consolidates several Windows administrative tools that you can use to manage the local PC or other computers on the network.
79	A	Microsoft Management Console is a Windows utility that can be used to build your own customized console windows.
80	D	A console is a single window that contains one or more administrative tools such as Device Manager or Disk Management.
81	A	Event Viewer is a Windows tool useful for troubleshooting problems with Windows, applications, and hardware.
82	C	In Event Viewer, the Application log records events about applications and Windows utilities, such as when an application was unable to open a file or when Windows created a restore point.
83	B	In Event Viewer, the System log records events triggered by Windows components, such as a device driver failing to load during the boot process or a problem with hardware.
84	D	In Event Viewer, the Set Up log records events about installing an application.
85	A	In Event Viewer, the Subscription log can be customized to collect certain events you require that are not normally collected by Event Viewer.
86	B	Event Viewer can be useful when you suspect someone is attempting to illegally log onto a system and you want to view login attempts, or the network is giving intermittent problems.
87	D	The Data Collector Sets utility can be used to collect your own data about the system.
88	C	The contributor permission allows you to write files and read existing files but not change existing files put there by others.
89	B	The co-owner permission allows you to have full control over the folder in the same way the owner does but is not identified as the folder owner.
90	A	Network Drive Map makes one PC (the client) appear to have a new hard drive, such as drive E, that is really hard drive space on another host computer (the server).
91	A	A computer that does nothing but provide hard drive storage on a network for other computers is called a file server or a network attached storage (NAS) device.

A

Question	Answer	Explanation
92	D	Vista startup is managed by two files: the Windows Boot Manager (BootMgr) and the Windows Boot Loader (WinLoad.exe).
93	B	BootMgr contains the partition table and the master boot program used to locate and start the BootMgr program.
94	D	The Boot Configuration Data (BCD) file is structured the same as a registry file and contains configuration information about how Vista is started.
95	A	The BCD file does not contain settings that detect device drivers.
96	C	Safe Mode boots the OS with a minimum configuration and can be used to solve problems with a new hardware installation or problems caused by user settings.
97	C	The Safe Mode with Networking option can be used when you are solving a problem with booting and need access to the network to solve the problem.
98	A	Registry settings collectively called the Last Known Good Configuration are saved in the registry each time the user successfully logs onto the system.
99	D	The debugging mode gives you the opportunity to move system boot logs from the failing computer to another computer for evaluation.
100	B	The Windows Vista Recovery Environment is an operating system launched from the Vista DVD that provides a graphical and command-line interface.

DOMAIN 4.0 NETWORKING

Question	Answer	Explanation
1	D	A PAN (personal area network) consists of personal devices at close range such as a cell phone, PDA, and notebook computer in communication.
2	B	A LAN (local area network) covers a small local area such as a home, office, other building, or small group of buildings.
3	C	A wireless LAN (WLAN) covers a limited geographical area and is popular where networking cables are difficult to install, such as outdoors, in public places, and in homes that are not wired for networks.
4	A	Bandwidth (the width of the band) is the theoretical number of bits that can be transmitted over a network at one time, similar to the number of lanes on a highway.
5	D	Delays in network transmissions are referred to as latency.

Question	Answer	Explanation
6	C	The Institute of Electrical and Electronics Engineers (IEEE) creates standards for computer and electronics industries.
7	A	TCP/IP is a group of protocols that control many different aspects of communication.
8	B	Before data is transmitted on a network, it is broken up into segments.
9	A	ISDN (Integrated Services Digital Network) is an outdated broadband technology developed in the 1980s that uses regular phone lines and is accessed by a dial-up connection.
10	C	Just as with cable TV, cable modems are always connected (always up).
11	A	Asymmetric DSL (ADSL) uses one upload speed from the consumer to an ISP and a faster download speed.
12	A	With cable modem, you share the TV cable infrastructure with your neighbors, which can result in service becoming degraded if many people in your neighborhood are using cable modems at the same time.
13	C	Fiber optic uses a dedicated line from your ISP to your place of business or residence.
14	A	The 802.11g and 802.11b standards use a frequency range of 2.4 GHz in the radio band and have a distance range of about 100 meters.
15	B	The 802.11n Wi-Fi standard uses multiple input/multiple output (MIMO) technology whereby two or more antennas are used at both ends of transmission.
16	D	The 802.11k standard defines how wireless network traffic can better be distributed over multiple access points covering a wide area so that the access point with the strongest signal is not overloaded.
17	A	WEP encryption is no longer considered secure.
18	C	A MAC (Media Access Control) address is a 6-byte number that uniquely identifies a network adapter on a computer.
19	A	WiMAX supports up to 75 Mbps with a range up to several miles and uses 2- to 11-GHz frequency.
20	A	GSM (Global System for Mobile Communications) is an open standard that uses digital communication of data and is accepted and used worldwide.
21	C	Bluetooth is a standard for short-range wireless communication and data synchronization between devices.
22	D	Dial-up networking works by using PPP (Point-to-Point Protocol) to send data packets over phone lines. PPP is, therefore, called a line protocol.

A

Question	Answer	Explanation
23	B	For a network port on the motherboard, a solid light indicates connectivity and a blinking light indicates activity.
24	C	The four speeds for Ethernet are 10 Mbps, 100 Mbps (Fast Ethernet), 1 Gbps (Gigabit Ethernet), and 10 Gbps (10-gigabit Ethernet).
25	C	CAT-6 has less crosstalk than CAT-5 or CAT-5e.
26	A	Coaxial cable has a single copper wire down the middle and a braided shield around it.
27	C	Fiber-optic cables transmit signals as pulses of light over glass strands inside protected tubing.
28	C	A single-mode cable uses a single path for light to travel in the cable.
29	B	Gigabit Ethernet is currently replacing 100BaseT Ethernet as the choice for LAN technology.
30	A	You can think of a hub as just a pass-through and distribution point for every device connected to it, without regard for what kind of data is passing through.
31	D	A switch is smarter and more efficient than a hub, as it keeps a table of all the devices connected to it. It uses this table to determine which path to use when sending packets.
32	C	A patch cable is used to connect a computer to a hub or switch.
33	D	A crossover cable is used to connect two like devices such as a switch to a switch or a PC to a PC.
34	D	A router is a device that manages traffic between two networks.
35	B	A DHCP (Dynamic Host Configuration Protocol) server gives IP addresses to computers on the network when they attempt to initiate a connection to the network and request an IP address.
36	A	NAT (Network Address Translation) is a protocol that substitutes the IP address of the router for the IP address of other computers inside the network when these computers need to communicate on the Internet.
37	C	At the root level of communication is hardware.
38	B	An OS is responsible for managing communication between itself and another computer, using rules for communication that both operating systems understand.
39	A	An IP address is a 32-bit string used to identify a computer on a network.
40	A	A network can use static IP addressing, in which each computer is assigned an IP address that never changes.
41	C	In dynamic IP addressing, each time the computer connects to the network, it gets a new IP address from the DHCP server.

Question	Answer	Explanation
42	B	When you use the Internet to surf the Web or download your e-mail, you are using an application on your computer called an Internet client.
43	D	You can address a Web server by entering into a browser address box an IP address followed by a colon and then the port number.
44	A	An intranet is a private network that uses the TCP/IP protocols.
45	A	The largest possible 8-bit number is 11111111, which is equal to 255 in decimal.
46	C	The first part of an IP address identifies the network.
47	B	The Internet Corporation for Assigned Names and Numbers (ICANN) is responsible for keeping track of assigned IP addresses and domain names.
48	A	Class D addresses begin with octets 224 through 239 and are used for multicasting, in which one host sends messages to multiple hosts, such as when the host transmits a video conference over the Internet.
49	C	Class E addresses begin with 240 through 254 and are reserved for research.
50	D	The subnet mask used in the TCP/IP configuration for a network tells the OS which part of an IP address is the network portion and which part identifies the host.
51	B	Subnet masks that contain all 1s or all 0s in an octet are called classful subnet masks.
52	D	The IP addresses available to the Internet are called public IP addresses.
53	D	Private IP addresses are IP addresses used on private intranets that are not allowed on the Internet.
54	B	When a workstation has an IP address assigned to it, it is said that the workstation is leasing the IP address.
55	C	A host name, also called a computer name, is the name of a computer and can be used in place of its IP address.
56	B	NetBIOS (Network Basic Input/Output System) is a protocol that applications use to communicate with each other.
57	A	A fully qualified domain name (FQDN) identifies a computer and the network to which it belongs.
58	C	On the Internet, a fully qualified domain name must be associated with an IP address before this computer can be found. This process of associating a character-based name with an IP address is called name resolution.
59	B	A DNS server can find an IP address for a computer when the fully qualified domain name is known.

A

Question	Answer	Explanation
60	D	When Windows is trying to resolve a computer name to an IP address, it first looks in the Hosts file in the C:\Windows\System32\drivers\etc folder.
61	A	HTTP (Hypertext Transfer Protocol) is the protocol used for the World Wide Web and used by Web browsers and Web servers to communicate.
62	C	The HTTPS (HTTP secure) protocol is used by Web browsers and servers to encrypt the data before it is sent and then decrypt it before the data is processed.
63	A	FTP (File Transfer Protocol) is used to transfer files between two computers.
64	D	SMTP AUTH is used to authenticate a user to an e-mail server when the e-mail client first tries to connect to the e-mail server to send e-mail.
65	C	The Telnet protocol is used by client/server applications to allow an administrator or other user to control a computer remotely.
66	B	In TCP/IP, the protocol that guarantees packet delivery is TCP (Transmission Control Protocol).
67	D	UDP is called a connectionless protocol or a best-effort protocol.
68	A	The Ping (Packet InterNet Groper) command tests connectivity by sending an echo request to a remote computer.
69	D	The Ipconfig command can display TCP/IP configuration information and refresh the IP address.
70	B	*Set localecho* displays command responses that are given by the remote computer.
71	D	The *Ctrl+]* command allows you to switch from the remote computer session mode window to the Telnet command mode window.
72	A	A VPN works by using encrypted data packets between a private network and a computer somewhere on the Internet.
73	C	A subnet mask is a group of four dotted decimal numbers such as 255.255.0.0 that tells TCP/IP if a computer's IP address is on the same or a different network.
74	A	A gateway is a computer or other device, such as a router, that allows a computer on one network to communicate with a computer on another network.
75	A	A default gateway is the gateway a computer uses to access another network if it does not have a better option.

DOMAIN 5.0 SECURITY

Question	Answer	Explanation
1	D	HIPAA includes regulations to secure patient data that applies to all health care companies and professionals.
2	C	NIST has published information technology standards for security to be followed by the U.S. government and its contractors.
3	B	The security plan should change with the organization.
4	D	Authentication proves that an individual is who he says he is and is accomplished by a variety of techniques, including a username, password, and personal identification number.
5	A	Authorization determines what an individual can do in the system after he is authenticated.
6	B	Because of the problem of losing encrypted data and Internet passwords when a user password is reset, each new user should create a password reset disk for use in the event he forgets the password.
7	A	Power-on passwords are assigned in BIOS setup and kept in CMOS RAM to prevent unauthorized access to the computer or to the BIOS setup utility.
8	C	Some notebooks give you the option of setting a hard drive password, which is set in BIOS setup and written on the hard drive. The name given to this type of password is drive lock password.
9	D	The protocols that encrypt account names and passwords are called authentication protocols.
10	C	The default protocol used by Windows Vista/XP is Kerberos.
11	D	Any small device that contains authentication information that can be keyed into a logon window by a user is called a smart card.
12	A	A digital certificate is assigned by a Certification Authority and is used to prove you are who you say you are.
13	A	A digital certificate is designed to help encrypt any data sent over the Internet to the corporate network, such as that used by a VPN.
14	B	A biometric device is an input device that inputs biological data about a person, which can identify a person's fingerprints, handprints, face, voice, eye, and handwritten signatures.
15	D	A strong password is one that is not easy to guess by humans and computer programs designed to hack passwords.
16	C	A passphrase is made of several words, with spaces allowed.
17	C	Don't use consecutive letters or numbers, such as "abcdefg" or "12345."

A

Question	Answer	Explanation
18	A	The Administrator account has complete access to the system and can make changes that affect the security of the system and other users.
19	C	The Standard account can use software and hardware and make some system changes, but it cannot make changes that affect the security of the system or other users.
20	A	The Guest account is not normally activated and has limited rights.
21	C	The Limited account has read-write access only on its own folders, read-only access to most system folders, and no access to other users' data.
22	B	Data classification involves putting data into categories and then deciding how secure each category must be.
23	A	The Encrypted File System works only when using Windows NTFS, the Windows Vista Ultimate and Business editions, and Windows XP Professional.
24	D	BitLocker Encryption locks down a hard drive by encrypting the entire Vista volume and any other volume on the drive.
25	A	Digital certificates are transported over the Internet and verified using the Public-Key Infrastructure.
26	C	The chip on the motherboard of many high-end computers is called the Trusted Platform Module chip.
27	D	To keep a system secure, users need to practice the habit of locking down their workstation each time they step away from their desks. The quickest way to do this is to press the Windows key and L.
28	A	Malicious software is an unwanted program that intends to harm you and is transmitted to your computer without your knowledge.
29	C	The term grayware describes any annoying and unwanted program that may or may not mean to harm you.
30	B	A virus is a program that replicates by attaching itself to other programs.
31	C	Adware is secretly installed on your computer when you download and install shareware or freeware, including screen savers, desktop wallpaper, music, cartoons, news, and weather alerts.
32	A	Spyware is software that installs itself on your computer to spy on you and to collect personal information about you.
33	B	Keylogger tracks all your keystrokes, including passwords, chat room sessions, e-mail messages, documents, online purchases, and anything else you type on your PC.
34	A	A program that copies itself throughout a network or the Internet without a host program is called a worm.

Question	Answer	Explanation
35	D	Junk e-mail that you do not want, you did not ask for, and that gets in your way is called spam.
36	C	Phishing is a type of identity theft where the sender of an e-mail message scams you into responding with personal data about yourself.
37	A	A dormant code added to software and triggered at a predetermined time or by a predetermined event is called a logic bomb.
38	D	A boot sector virus hides in either of two boot sectors of a hard drive.
39	B	A small program contained in a document that can be automatically executed either when the document is first loaded or later by pressing a key combination is called a macro.
40	A	Social engineering is the practice of tricking people into giving out private information or allowing unsafe programs into the network or computer.

DOMAIN 6.0 OPERATIONAL PROCEDURE

Question	Answer	Explanation
1	B	The Materials Safety Data Sheet explains how to properly handle substances such as chemical solvents.
2	D	The MSDS includes information such as physical data, toxicity, health effects, first aid, storage, shipping, disposal, and spill procedures.
3	A	You should dispose of these batteries in the regular trash.
4	B	You should dispose of them by returning them to the original dealer or by taking them to a recycling center.
5	D	Purchase insurance on the shipment. Postal insurance is not expensive, and it can save you a lot of money if materials are damaged in transit.
6	D	Speak politely and use language that won't confuse your customer. Avoid using slang or jargon (technical language that only technical people can understand).
7	D	It is not recommended that you concentrate on technical skills and ignore interpersonal skills.
8	B	You should never use the phone without permission.
9	C	You should never make assumptions.
10	D	Troubleshooting begins by interviewing the user.

A

Question	Answer	Explanation
11	A	Use diplomacy and good manners when you work with a user to solve a problem. For example, if you suspect that the user dropped the PC, don't ask, "Did you drop the PC?" Put the question in a less accusatory manner: "Could the PC have been dropped?"
12	B	You should not complain about your job, your boss or coworkers, your company, or other companies or products to your customers.
13	A	A help desk call is the most difficult situation to handle when a customer is not knowledgeable about how to use a computer.
14	C	Don't be defensive. It's better to leave the customer with the impression that you and your company are listening and willing to admit mistakes.
15	B	Allow the customer enough time to be fully satisfied that all is working. Does the printer work? Print a test page. Does the network connection work? Can the customer log on to the network and access data on it?
16	C	Not all power strips are surge suppressors.
17	D	For onsite support, a customer expects documentation about your services.
18	B	A professional puts business matters above personal matters.
19	A	A capacitor holds its charge even after the power is turned off and the device is unplugged.
20	C	A ground is the easiest possible path for electricity to follow.
21	B	Both the power supply and monitor are considered to be a field replaceable unit (FRU).
22	A	Electrostatic discharge (ESD), commonly known as static electricity, is an electrical charge at rest.
23	C	An ungrounded conductor (such as wire that is not touching another wire) or a nonconductive surface (such as your hair) holds a charge until the charge is released.
24	D	A catastrophic failure destroys the component beyond use. An upset failure damages the component so that it does not perform well, even though it may still function to some degree.
25	A	A ground bracelet contains a resistor that prevents electricity from harming you.
26	B	Ground mats dissipate ESD and are commonly used by bench technicians (also called depot technicians) who repair and assemble computers at their workbenches or in an assembly line.
27	D	A Faraday cage is any device that protects against an electromagnetic field.

Question	Answer	Explanation
28	B	Antistatic gloves are designed to prevent ESD between you and a device as you pick it up and handle it.
29	A	Electromagnetic interference is caused by the magnetic field produced as a side effect when electricity flows.
30	D	Antistatic gloves can be substituted for an antistatic bracelet and are good for moving, packing, or unpacking sensitive equipment.
31	D	Data in data cables that cross an electromagnetic field or that run parallel with power cables can become corrupted by EMI/RFI. This causes crosstalk.
32	A	Crosstalk can be partially controlled by using data cables covered with a protective material. These cables are called shielded cables.
33	D	A surge protector protects equipment against sudden changes in power level, such as spikes from lightning strikes.
34	C	One joule is the work or energy required to produce one watt of power in one second.
35	B	A suppressor is rated as to the amount of joules it can expend before it no longer can work to protect the circuit from the power surge.
36	B	A clamping voltage is the voltage point at which a suppressor begins to absorb or block voltage.
37	D	In addition to providing protection against spikes, line conditioners, also called power conditioners, regulate, or condition, the power, providing continuous voltage during brownouts.
38	A	The uninterruptible power supply (UPS) provides backup power in the event that the AC fails completely.
39	C	VA is the theoretical rating that is calculated by multiplying volts by amps and then added up for all the equipment.
40	D	Do not place or store expansion cards on top of or next to a CRT monitor, which can discharge as much as 29,000 volts onto the screen.
41	C	The best way to guard against ESD is to use a ground bracelet together with a ground mat.
42	C	Generally, do not work on a computer if you or the computer have just come in from the cold, because there is more danger of ESD when the atmosphere is cold and dry.
43	A	LCD monitors do not emit EMI/RFI.
44	D	If mysterious, intermittent errors persist on a PC, one thing to suspect is EMI/RFI.

A

Question	Answer	Explanation
45	B	The UL standard that applies to surge suppressors is UL 1449, first published in 1985 and revised in 1998.
46	A	Surge suppressors can come as power strips, wall-mounted units that plug into AC outlets, or consoles designed to sit beneath the monitor on a desktop.
47	C	When passing a circuit board, memory module, or other sensitive component to another person, ground yourself and then touch the other person before you pass the component.
48	B	To help cut down on EMI between PCs, always install face plates in empty drive bays or slot covers over empty expansion slots.
49	A	A simple way to detect EMI is to use an inexpensive AM radio.
50	D	If EMI in the electrical circuits coming to the PC causes a significant problem, you can use a line conditioner to filter the electrical noise that causes the EMI.

1.0–4.0

COMPTIA A+ 220-702
PRACTICAL APPLICATIONS
EXAM ANSWERS

DOMAIN 1.0 HARDWARE

Question	Answer	Explanation
1	C	It is essential to make sure the form factor of the power supply, motherboard, and case all match, so that they fit and work together. The processor and motherboard must also be compatible, but this is not an aspect of the form factor.
2	B	A power supply produces slightly higher wattage at room temperature (peak) than once the temperature inside the case has risen (continuous).
3	A	Typically, the video card draws the most power.
4	B	The motherboard and processor will use about 150W, the PCI card 20W, the hard drives about 35W each, the tape drive and the CD drive about 25W each, the low-end video card about 40W, and the fans about 5W each, all including about 30% extra headroom, totaling 415W.
5	D	The two high-end video cards use a lot of power, up to 300W or so each. Add 35W each for the two hard drives and the two optical drives, and 5W each for the fans, and the total is over 900W.
6	A	We can get away with a smaller power supply for this system: 100W for the motherboard and processor, another 100W for the video card, 25W for the hard drive, 35W for the DVD drive, and 5W for the fan. 300W should be fine, perhaps even generous.
7	B	The dangers of ESD are higher when the air is cold and dry.
8	B	A power supply tester is used to measure the output of each connector coming from the power supply.

B

Question	Answer	Explanation
9	D	To match pins on one end of a cable to pins on the other end, use continuity mode.
10	D	Such high-voltage devices can contain enough power to kill you, even when unplugged, and should only be opened by someone specifically trained to do so.
11	D	All of these are important, but the *first* step is often to make a backup.
12	A	A floppy drive cable is a ribbon cable with a 34-pin connector and a twist in the cable.
13	C	Install the power supply first, and install the motherboard in the case before installing cards in the motherboard.
14	B	Powering all the way down suggests that the issue is power- or heat-related, and because the problem occurs when the computer has been working for several hours, heat is the most likely cause.
15	C	The problem might be due to insufficient wattage. You want to replace the power supply with one with *at least as high* a wattage rating. Add up the wattage requirements of all the components to be sure.
16	D	Faulty power supplies can cause all kinds of problems, including all of these.
17	B	A POST diagnostic tool is useful when troubleshooting startup errors caused by hardware.
18	B	An AM radio tuned to a low frequency will play static in the presence of EMI.
19	A	Of the form factors listed, full-size ATX has the largest motherboard.
20	B	CMOS RAM holds configuration data and is powered by a small battery on the motherboard.
21	A	The motherboard determines many of the system's other features.
22	D	Monitoring CPU temperature is more likely handled by driver software installed to the OS.
23	B	An expression BIOS update is done by downloading and running an application from Windows.
24	C	Most motherboards have a group of BIOS jumpers that can be used to recover from a failed BIOS update or forgotten power-on password.
25	C	Most manufacturers say to install the motherboard in the case first because the cooler is heavy, but some suggest the other order.
26	D	The CPU fan is connected to pins on the motherboard, typically labeled something like "CPU Fan Header."

Question	Answer	Explanation
27	A	Access the BIOS setup program by pressing a key or combination of keys during the boot process.
28	C	The order is called the "boot sequence."
29	B	AGP is used solely for video cards.
30	B	Disabling the network port and installing a network expansion card is the best solution.
31	A	Form factor is determined by the motherboard, but it does not directly constrain the choice of processor.
32	B	Apply just enough thermal compound to create a thin layer over the surface.
33	C	The mostly likely problem is that the processor is not seated correctly or some power cord is not correctly connected.
34	B	The processor is probably overheating because the cooler is not correctly installed.
35	A	Hold a processor by the edges, being careful not to touch the surfaces of the processor.
36	C	Put thermal compound on either the bottom of the cooler or the top of the processor, but not both.
37	D	The installation procedure varies slightly for each socket type and even for each motherboard and cooler, but the process is largely the same for Intel and AMD processors.
38	D	The S4 state is called hibernation and shuts the system down after writing everything in RAM to a special file on the hard drive.
39	D	Higher P state values have lower frequencies.
40	D	EIST and PowerNow! Implement ACPI P states.
41	C	S3 suspends to RAM.
42	D	The deeper the C state, the longer it takes the processor to wake up.
43	B	A power supply may whine if too much power is being drawn.
44	C	If nothing happens at all, the system doesn't have time to overheat, and something else (perhaps power) is the problem.
45	A	The temperature should not exceed 100° F (38° C).
46	B	Generally, rear case fans are exhaust fans, pulling warm air out of the case.
47	C	If a case is equipped with a front case fan, it is typically intended to pull cold air into the case.
48	B	Most triple-channel boards revert to dual-channel if four DIMMs are installed, although some may revert to single channeling.

B

Question	Answer	Explanation
49	C	Installing an identical DIMM in each of the first three slots will allow triple channeling.
50	B	If you mix memory speeds, all modules will perform at the slowest speed.
51	D	Buffered and unbuffered memory can't be mixed.
52	A	DIMMs are installed straight down.
53	A	A 32-bit OS can address only up to 4 GB of RAM.
54	B	Laptops typically take Small Outline dual inline memory modules.
55	C	You'll probably get full capacity, but only at single channeling.
56	C	The fourth pin controls pulse width modulation, allowing the motherboard to vary the fan's speed.
57	A	Any of these are possibilities, but given the symptoms and the fact that high-performance video cards generate a lot of heat, overheating is the most likely.
58	B	DIMM slots in matched pairs suggests dual-channel memory.
59	B	Three DIMM slots of the same color suggests triple-channel memory.
60	B	Identical DIMMs in the first three slots will enable triple-channel memory access.
61	C	For dual-channel memory access, matched pairs should be installed in the matching slots.
62	A	Enter 'Msinfo32' to bring up the System Information window.
63	C	The three colored slots suggest triple-channeling, which is only supported by DDR3 DIMMs.
64	B	SATA is the most likely choice for the hard drive.
65	C	An expansion card that provides a SATA interface is the best solution.
66	A	SATA drives do not generally need to have jumpers set.
67	B	For Windows, NTFS is usually the best choice for the file system of a new hard drive and is always available.
68	A	The blue end connects to the motherboard.
69	B	If only one drive is connected to the cable, put it on the black connector at the end.
70	A	The hard drive should be configured to be the master.
71	B	Place the faster devices on the primary channel to avoid being slowed down by slower devices.
72	B	The hard drive should get the primary channel to itself.

Question	Answer	Explanation
73	A	The fastest hard drive should be the boot device and the only device on the primary channel.
74	D	Cable-select requires a cable-select data cable.
75	B	3.5-inch hard drives are about the same size as floppy disk drives.
76	C	A universal bay kit adapter allows a hard drive to be installed into a wider bay.
77	D	RAID can be implemented on many motherboards, with a RAID controller card, or in software.
78	D	Motherboard-based hardware RAID is enabled in the BIOS setup.
79	C	The end with the twist connects to the drive; the colored edge indicates pin 1.
80	C	Begin by attempting to mount the drive in another system to copy the data off of it before attempting to solve the original problem.
81	D	The bootloader does not enter the equation until after POST.
82	C	If you can boot using another medium, the problem is isolated to the hard drive subsystem.
83	B	One of the worst things you can do for a drive that is having difficulty starting up is to leave the computer turned off for an extended period of time.
84	A	This error occurs when trying to boot from a nonbootable disk.
85	C	A drive can only be replaced without powering down if it is hot-swappable.
86	A	RAID 0 (striping) is most appropriate in this case.
87	B	RAID 1 (mirroring) is most appropriate in this case.
88	D	RAID 5 is the best choice in this case.
89	A	Blue indicates the primary channel.
90	C	This is the easiest thing to check, so try it first.
91	B	You just need a bay adapter; the interface and BIOS should work the same.
92	B	This is done in BIOS setup.
93	C	Begin by making sure Windows recognizes the port.
94	B	A shorter PCIe card will work in a longer PCIe slot.
95	A	PCI cards should be pushed straight down into the slot.
96	A	Whining suggests the card is not getting enough power.
97	B	The onboard video port is likely not disabled.
98	C	BIOS cannot detect a video card.

B

Question	Answer	Explanation
99	D	This is a symptom of outdated drivers.
100	D	It is good practice to check a suspected-defective cable again to make sure the problem was not simply the connection.
101	B	The Found New Hardware Wizard should launch.
102	B	Plug a single connector into the green port.
103	C	Card readers usually connect to an internal USB header on the motherboard.
104	D	Windows XP does not include software to burn DVDs.
105	A	Start by checking whether Windows Device Manager reports problems.
106	D	Check the status indicator lights first.
107	B	The standard size for a notebook hard drive is 2.5 inches.
108	D	One of the difficulties of servicing notebook computers is their variability.
109	A	The MiniPCIe slot is smaller than the MiniPCI slot, and the MiniPCI slot has clips to hold in the card, which the MiniPCIe slot does not have.
110	B	Bluetooth 2.0 is faster than Bluetooth 1.0 and uses less power.
111	B	If the screen is dim but you can make out that some display is present, the problem might be the video inverter, which interfaces between the LCD panel and the motherboard.
112	D	Always be sure to remove both the AC adapter and the battery before servicing a notebook computer.
113	D	Maintenance procedures vary from printer to printer.
114	C	Remove the toner cartridge and gently rock it from side to side to redistribute the toner.

DOMAIN 2.0 OPERATING SYSTEMS

Question	Answer	Explanation
1	B	Two beeps followed by three, four, or five beeps most often means there are errors in the first 64 KB of RAM.
2	C	Three beeps followed by two, three, or four beeps most often means an embedded keyboard or video controller failed.
3	D	One beep followed by three, four, or five beeps indicates a motherboard problem, probably fatal.

Question	Answer	Explanation
4	C	The BIOS has successfully completed POST, which includes a test of the video card.
5	A	An ECC_ERROR indicates a problem with RAM.
6	B	BOOTMGR is the bootloading program for the OS.
7	C	CMOS RAM contains the BIOS setup.
8	D	All of these are signs of failing capacitors, which generally means the motherboard needs to be replaced.
9	A	Devices can be uninstalled from the Device Manager.
10	A	Windows Vista stores user directories in C:\Users\.
11	C	Windows XP stores user directories in C:\Documents and Settings\.
12	A	Program files are generally stored in C:\Program Files.
13	D	On 64-bit systems, 32-bit programs are stored in C:\Program Files (x86). The x86 refers to a somewhat vestigial name for the 32-bit processor architecture.
14	A	Native program files are stored in C:\Program Files.
15	A	In Windows Vista, Internet Explorer's temporary files are stored in C:\Users*username*\AppData\Local\Microsoft\Windows\Temporary Internet Files.
16	C	In Windows XP, Internet Explorer's temporary files are stored in C:\Documents and Settings*username*\Local Settings\Temporary Internet Files.
17	C	Run cmd.exe to get a command prompt.
18	A	Copy /a copies only those files that have changed since the last backup.
19	B	The md command makes a directory.
20	B	The /r switch causes chkdsk to check for bad sectors.
21	B	Defrag defragments the file system.
22	B	A file system should be defragmented about once a week.
23	B	The Edit program is a simple command-line text editor.
24	C	Notepad saves files in plain ASCII format, which is appropriate for batch files.
25	D	All of these methods can be used to format a disk.
26	A	Create a mounted drive with C:\Users as the mount point.
27	A	Windows Vista Home Edition does not support dynamic disks.
28	D	Mirroring using dynamic disks is not available in Windows Vista.

B

Question	Answer	Explanation
29	C	A dynamic disk requires 1 MB of storage at the end of the disk for the disk management database.
30	C	Active means the volume is the one BIOS looks to for an OS.
31	A	Healthy indicates that the volume is formatted with a file system and that the file system is working without errors.
32	B	Online status indicates the disk has been sensed by Windows and can be accessed by either reading or writing to the disk.
33	C	If you move a hard drive that has been configured as a dynamic disk on another computer to this computer, this computer will report the disk as a foreign drive.
34	C	Hardware RAID is preferable for both of these reasons.
35	B	Only Windows Vista Ultimate Edition allows language packs to be downloaded via Windows Update.
36	C	If the user assures you that no information, data, or settings are needed from the old Windows installation, it's safe to delete these files.
37	B	Always store important data on more than one medium.
38	A	It may seem mundane, but the first things to do to improve performance are routine maintenance tasks.
39	D	Windows Experience Index is a summary index designed to measure the overall performance of a system.
40	A	The Advanced Tools window, from the Windows Experience Index, shows performance issues and tools that could help.
41	C	The Reliability Monitor in the Reliability and Performance Monitor provides a graph of system stability over time, since Windows was installed.
42	C	If you notice that performance slows after a system has been up and running without a restart for some time, suspect a memory leak.
43	B	You see the greatest performance increase using ReadyBoost when you have a slow hard drive (running at less than 7200 RPM).
44	B	XP's disk defragmenter does not have an option to run every week, but this can be set up using the Task Scheduler.
45	B	Although the others can be temporarily disabled to identify a problem, all perform important functions.
46	D	All of these are important clean-up steps after manually deleting program files.
47	D	Task Manager is useful to stop a process that is hung.
48	C	Msconfig can be used to temporarily disable startup processes.

Question	Answer	Explanation
49	C	Msconfig can be used to find a startup program causing a problem.
50	B	The Services console is used to manage services.
51	A	If the system's performance improves when booted in Safe Mode, nonessential startup programs are slowing down the system when Windows starts normally.
52	C	If the performance problem still exists in Safe Mode, you can assume that the problem is with a hardware device, a critical driver, or a Windows component.
53	D	If you observe that the values in these three columns increase over time for a particular program, suspect the program has a memory leak.
54	A	First run Msconfig to get information about the problem.
55	B	For essential hardware devices, use the System File Checker (SFC) to verify and replace system files.
56	A	Updating the device drivers is often a first step when troubleshooting a problem with a device driver.
57	B	After you have made a change, be sure to restart and check to see if the problem is resolved before you move on to the next step.
58	D	Interviewing the user and backing up data if necessary are almost always the first steps to solving a problem.
59	B	If you can identify the approximate date the error started and that date is in the recent past, use System Restore. This can solve problems with registry entries the application uses that have become corrupted.
60	C	If the application works in Safe Mode, you can assume the problem is not with the application but with the operating system, device drivers, or other applications that load at startup and that are conflicting with the application.
61	A	Any problems that occur before the progress bar appears are most likely related to corrupt or missing system files or hardware.
62	C	Your best Vista tools for these problems are Startup Repair and System Restore.
63	B	After the progress bar appears, user mode services and drivers are loaded, and then the logon screen appears.
64	D	Problems with these components can best be solved using Startup Repair, the Last Known Good Configuration, System Restore, Safe Mode, Device Manager, and Msconfig.
65	C	After the logon screen appears, problems can be caused by startup scripts, applications set to launch at startup, and desktop settings.

B

Question	Answer	Explanation
66	A	Use Msconfig to temporarily disable startup programs.
67	A	This error message indicates that BIOS could not find a hard drive.
68	B	This error message indicates that BIOS was able to find the hard drive but couldn't read it or couldn't find what it was looking for.
70	D	This error indicates that BIOS could not find the hard drive.
71	A	It can't do any harm, it's easy to use, and it might fix the problem.
72	D	System Restore, Safe Mode, and Device Manager are useful for fixing a problem with a device or its drivers.
73	B	Problem Reports and Solutions, Reliability and Performance Monitor, and Event Viewer are useful for identifying which device is causing a problem.
74	B	Task Manager, Problem Reports and Solutions, and Windows updates can help with troubleshooting an application problem.
75	A	Safe Mode, Last Known Good Configuration, and Startup Repair can help with troubleshooting a failed boot.
76	C	If a hard drive contains valuable data but will not boot, you might be able to recover the data by installing the drive in another system as the second, nonbooting hard drive.
77	B	Mdsched.exe launches the Memory Diagnostics tool.
78	A	Use the Device Manager to uninstall a USB device.
79	A	The Device Manager is also the appropriate tool for uninstalling a device in Windows XP.
80	A	Use the Device Manager to uninstall a network card.
81	B	System Restore restores the Windows system to a previous point in time.
82	A	The Device Manager can also be used to update drivers.
83	B	Startup Repair can sometimes fix drastic problems with system files and boot records.
84	A	The volume on which Windows is installed is formatted and then restored from the most recent backup.
85	A	The file Ntuser.dat in the user's folder contains these settings.
86	C	If you need an elevated Command Prompt window in Vista, click Start, All Programs, and Accessories and right-click Command Prompt. Then select Run as Administrator from the shortcut window.
87	D	The ? character has a special meaning at the command line. (It is a wildcard.)
88	C	Ipconfig /release releases the current IP address; Ipconfig /renew requests a new one.

Question	Answer	Explanation
89	C	The * character has a special meaning at the command line. (It is a wild-card.)
90	A	For example: net use z: \\computername\folder
91	A	Microsoft encourages you to put files in this Public folder that will be shared on the network so that your private user data folders are better protected.
92	B	Windows stores the registry in C:\Windows\system32\config.
93	C	Use the Dir command to list files and directories.
94	D	Either del or erase will delete a file.
95	C	A drive may have one, two, or three primary partitions, as well as an extended partition.
96	C	User startup items are stored in C:\Users\UserName\AppData\Roaming\Microsoft\Windows\Start Menu\Programs\Startup.
97	A	Vista Home and Vista Starter do not include Complete PC Backup.
98	C	Make sure at least 15 percent of drive C is free.
99	B	Use Ntbackup in Windows XP to back up the system state.
100	B	To be used for ReadyBoost, a flash device must have at least 256 MB free and have a throughput of at least 2 MB/s.
101	C	Moving Pagefile.sys can help if the new disk is faster and there is enough room (three or four times the RAM size) on the new disk.
102	A	The client-side cache is located at C:\Windows\CSC.

DOMAIN 3.0 NETWORKING

Question	Answer	Explanation
1	C	Use the jack that connects directly to the point where the cable comes into the house, with no splitters between the jack and entrance point.
2	D	Cable modems may connect to the PC through Ethernet (also referred to as patch or network) or USB.
3	B	The cable company needs to know the MAC address of the cable modem.
4	A	To prevent static on the line, install a telephone filter on every phone jack in the house that is being used by a telephone, fax machine, or dial-up modem.
5	C	An on-demand broadband connection is managed by PPPoE.

B

Question	Answer	Explanation
6	B	A hardware firewall is used to protect all computers on the network from malicious activity coming from the Internet.
7	D	All of these contain a firewall.
8	A	A public profile offers the highest level of protection when you are connected to a public network.
9	C	The least protection is used for a domain profile, when your PC is on a domain and security is managed by the domain's operating system.
10	B	The maximum recommended length of an Ethernet cable is 100 meters.
11	A	An Ethernet switch simply connects multiple computers by way of Ethernet patch cables.
12	C	Place the wireless access point near the center of the area where you want your wireless network.
13	A	The wireless access point and computers connect to the switch, which connects to the router, which connects to the cable modem, which connects to the ISP. (Often the router, switch, and wireless access point are all integrated into a wireless router.)
14	C	When you first install a router, before you do anything else, change your router password.
15	D	For the server to always be available, it needs an IP address that is known and does not change.
16	C	Port filtering is used to open or close ports so they cannot be used.
17	B	Port forwarding means that the firewall forwards traffic on a specific port to a specific computer on the network.
18	A	Port triggering opens a port when a PC on the network initiates communication on another port.
19	B	Your network must have a static IP so that your router can always be reached at the same address. Most cable companies charge an additional fee for a static IP.
20	D	MAC filtering allows you to limit access to a whitelist of computers, identified by their MAC address.
21	C	DHCP allows you to limit the number of computers connected at once by limiting the range of dynamic IP addresses distributed.
22	A	The wireless network's name is called its SSID.
23	B	Getmac displays the NIC's MAC address.
24	C	Nslookup displays information about domain names and their IP addresses.

Question	Answer	Explanation
25	B	Netstat displays information about current TCP/IP connections.
26	C	Ipconfig /release releases the current IP address; Ipconfig /renew requests a new one.
27	C	Telnet allows you to communicate with another computer on the network remotely.
28	D	Tracert traces and displays the route taken from the host to a remote destination.
29	C	To use Remote Desktop, the computer you want to remotely access (the server) must be running Vista Business or Ultimate or Windows XP Professional.
30	B	Remote Assistance allows a user to send an invitation to see her desktop and, with permission, take control of her computer.
31	A	This is the easiest way to start a Remote Assistance session.
32	A	Troubleshooting problems with networking starts at the bottom layer (hardware) and proceeds to the top layer (applications).
33	D	Begin by trying to release and renew the IP address.
34	D	127.0.0.1 is the loopback address, which always refers to your computer.
35	C	If you get an error, assume that the problem is on your PC.
36	A	Use the netstat command with the –b parameter to help you find this program.
37	D	This suggests a problem with name resolution, either in the Hosts file or the DNS system.
38	B	Satellite Internet access in North America uses a satellite dish that faces the southern sky.
39	C	For fastest speeds, make sure all devices on the network use 1000BaseT.
40	C	WEP is older and might be the only choice on older hardware.
41	A	For example: net use z: \\computername\folder
42	C	SMTP is an outgoing mail transfer protocol.
43	C	Always check the simplest things first, and always start with hardware and work up.
44	D	Use the File Sharing dialog box in Windows Vista to share files and folders.
45	B	SSH uses port 22.

B

DOMAIN 4.0 SECURITY

Question	Answer	Explanation
1	C	The Power User group is available only in Windows XP.
2	B	When you create a folder or file that is not part of your user profile, by default, Windows gives access to all authenticated users.
3	B	The Everyone group includes the Authenticated Users group as well as the Guest account.
4	C	For Windows XP, to disable simple file sharing, open the Folder Options applet in the Control Panel and click the View tab of the Folder Options box; then scroll down to the bottom of the Advanced settings list, uncheck Use Simple File Sharing (Recommended), and click Apply.
5	D	Permissions are probably being inherited from Windows default or from the parent folder.
6	D	To turn off permissions inheritance, right-click the folder in question, select Properties, Security, Advanced and uncheck the box for inheriting permissions.
7	A	File and Printer Sharing for Microsoft Networks, File Sharing, and Public Folder Sharing must all be turned on.
8	C	Both username and password must match, or the user will be considered an anonymous user.
9	C	If you want to share a folder but don't want others to see the shared folder in their Network or My Network Places window, add a $ to the end of the folder name.
10	D	Vista Ultimate, Vista Business, and XP Professional allow for encrypting a file or folder.
11	C	Encrypted files or folders are displayed in Explorer in green.
12	A	Certificates are managed using the Certificate Manager console.
13	A	To allow other local users access to your encrypted files, you need to add another user's certificate to your encrypted file.
14	D	You cannot share an encrypted file on the network unless the computer belongs to a Windows domain.
15	B	EFS encryption cannot be used to encrypt Windows system files.
16	C	BitLocker can provide either computer authentication, user authentication, or both.
17	C	Immediately disconnect the suspected computer from other computers on your network so the virus cannot spread.

Question	Answer	Explanation
18	C	When AV software is not already installed on an infected computer, the most effective way to clean the computer is to run AV software from another computer.
19	C	Windows does not always allow AV software to look in this storage area. Unless you desperately need to keep a restore point, the best idea is to purge all restore points.
20	D	If you spot an Svchost.exe process running under a username, suspect a rat.
21	B	Svchost.exe is located in C:\Windows\system32\.
22	D	Winlogon.exe is located in C:\Windows\system32\.
23	B	When setting up local shares for multiple users who have similar job needs, it is easier to assign permissions to user groups than to individual users.
24	A	Explicit permissions override inherited permissions.
25	B	Share permissions apply to remote users of a file or folder.
26	B	Administrative shares are automatically set up if the computer is in a domain.
27	C	These administrative shares to each volume on a domain are also enabled by default.
28	B	To use BitLocker to authenticate the computer, the computer needs a TPM chip to hold the encryption key.
29	D	The best way to change inherited permissions is to change the permissions of the parent object.
30	B	Enter certmgr.msc to launch the Certificate Manager.
31	C	.pfx files contain the certificate and your private key. You should export a .cer file, which does not contain the private key.
32	D	If the Encrypt Contents to Secure Data check box is dimmed on the Advanced Attributes box, know that this version of Windows does not support encryption.
33	B	If the Advanced button is missing on the General tab of a file or folder properties box, know that the volume is not using NTFS.
34	A	All these symptoms suggest that malicious software is at work.
35	B	The primary danger of BitLocker encryption is the risk of losing all copies of the startup key.
36	C	The drive lock password is stored on the hard drive so that it will still control access to the drive if the drive is removed from the computer and installed in another system.

B

Question	Answer	Explanation
37	B	If your computer goes into hibernation while the file is open, a criminal might later be able to read the data in the Pagefile.sys file by booting the system from another OS.
38	B	Use the BIOS reset jumpers on the motherboard.
39	B	In the Vista Start Search box, enter tpm.msc.

Penoldt
Adam
Kelly
Katie

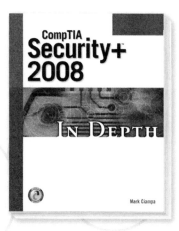

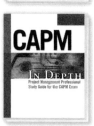